CUSTOMIZE

your HP-28

E. W. GIRARD

by

W.A.C. Mier-Jędrzejowicz, Ph.D.

"Customize your HP-28" by W.A.C. Mier-Jędrzejowicz, Ph.D.
First printing June 1988

ISBN 0 9510733 1 1

Library of Congress Card Catalogue Number : 88-090895

Published by:
W.A.C. Mier-Jędrzejowicz
40, Heathfield Road
London W3 8EJ
United Kingdom

United States publishers:
SYNTHETIX
P.O. Box 1080
Berkeley, CA 94701-1080
U.S.A.

Write to the above addresses for price information.
Please enclose an addressed envelope for reply.

Copyright 1988, W.A.C. Mier-Jędrzejowicz

INTRODUCTION

When they announced the HP-28C, Hewlett-Packard said they had reinvented the calculator. This seems to be a well justified description. As with most inventions though, the inventors could not foresee all its uses, nor all the problems that would show up.

Many problems and difficulties found by users can be summed up in the question "How can I make it behave exactly the way I want it to behave?" This book is written to answer that sort of question - it tells you how you can arrange for your HP-28 to behave more closely to the way you wish - in other words how to "customize" it.

There are five chapters, subdivided into specific points, and five appendices. The first two chapters have suggestions on fairly simple things, such as setting modes and creating variables. The third describes things which can be done with the special instruction SYSEVAL. The fourth shows some ways in which control of the HP-28 can be extended still further by machine language programming. Chapter five shows how you can customize the HP-28 by modifying its hardware - in particular by adding more memory to an HP-28C. The appendices deal with additional special topics.

The information in the first two chapters and the first two appendices is easy to understand and will be of interest to all HP-28 users. The subsequent chapters and appendices can be left for later reading.

Many of the suggestions have been published in the regular HP-28 NOTES column of DATAFILE, the magazine of HPCC, the British club for users of HP handheld calculators and computers. My original reason for writing this book was to provide members of HPCC with information that could not be fitted into "HP-28 Notes".

Two types of customization dealt with in particular are ways to make the HP-28 behave more like an HP-41 and ways to make its language more similar to FORTH. Many HPCC members wanted to transfer some of their HP-41 programs to an HP-28, so customization of the HP-28 to let it provide commands similar to ones on an HP-41 is an important subject. Some of the suggestions in this book come from ideas already discussed in relation to the HP-41 or other HP calculators, but a lot has come from ideas suggested by members of HP user clubs. This book is written for all those people, with my sincere thanks to everyone who has helped with suggestions and questions; where possible I have acknowledged the originators of ideas. I want to express my thanks to Tony Collinson of HP UK for keeping me up to date on HP-28 matters, to Kim Holm in Denmark for enthusiastically supporting my ideas, and especially to Dr. Bill Wickes, the master himself. I am particularly grateful to Colin Crowther, Frans de Vries and especially Bruce Bailey for their proofreading. My thanks go as ever to my Mother for helping while I wrote.

The new **HP-28S** has additional features not provided by the HP-28C. Some details are given in Appendix E, but programs written for the HP-28C will work on an HP-28S too. In places I have shown how an HP-28C can be provided with some of the additional HP-28S features.

Indeed the HP-28 provides a whole range of features which had never previously been available on one calculator.

WARNING: Chapter Three of this book deals with the use of the SYSEVAL command. Use of the SYSEVAL command in these ways is not supported by Hewlett-Packard, making this a NOMAS (Not MAnufacturer Supported) feature. As on all NOMAS features do <u>not</u> call Hewlett-Packard with questions about this. Also be aware that unpredictable behavior of the calculator is possible when using NOMAS features.

CONTENTS

Page

Special HP-28 Keys and Symbols   ix

CHAPTER 1. TIPS, KEYS AND MODES   1

1.1 Read the manuals   1
1.2 Do some examples   1
1.3 Keep notes   1
1.4 Practice makes perfect   2
1.5 Useful keys   3
1.6 Useful key combinations   3
1.7 What is a mode?   5
1.8 Check your modes with PRMD   6
1.9 Learn to use the modes   7
1.10 LAST, UNDO and COMMAND   7
1.11 A detailed look at LAST   8
1.12 More about UNDO and COMMAND   9
1.13 A look at the command line   11
1.14 About ENTER   13
1.15 Other modes   15
1.16 Create your own modes   15
1.17 Using the printer control flags   16

CHAPTER 2. VARIABLES, PROGRAMS AND MENUS   17

2.1 Simple constants   17
2.2 Simple variables   18
2.3 Commands or variables?   19
2.4 Variables and programs   20

2.5 COMMAND and programs   21

2.6 Simple programs   23

2.7 Longer programs   25

2.8 Algebraic expressions   28

2.9 Writing and testing programs   30

2.10 Some space saving tips   32

2.11 Subprograms and routines   33

2.12 Set your modes   35

2.13 Putting non-keyable characters in programs   36

2.14 Subprograms and local variables   38

2.15 Complex numbers and arrays   42

2.16 Algebra with binary numbers   42

2.17 Storing data in numbered registers and the stack   43

2.18 Tidying up memory and the USER menu   45

2.19 Playing with menus   46

2.20 One-command programs   46

CHAPTER 3. USING SYSEVAL   47

3.1 Version numbers   47

3.2 The system clock   48

3.3 A programmable SHIFT   53

3.4 A bit more memory?   54

3.5 Playing with SYSEVAL   54

3.6 A generalized STO   56

3.7 Programming with UNDO and COMMAND   59

3.8 'BIP' and error messages   61

3.9 Non-Normalized numbers and more about SYSEVAL   63

3.10 Non-Normalized objects, and a programmable CONT   68
    and SST

3.11 Program control of menus   74

3.12 A NAME command   77

3.13 Using EDIT in your programs   78

CHAPTER 4. MACHINE LANGUAGE PROGRAMMING   81

4.1 The layout of programs   81
4.2 Copyrights and copy wrongs   87
4.3 A simple machine language program   90
4.4 A PEEK command   93
4.5 Playing with PEEK   100
4.6 And now a POKE command   102
4.7 Jumping to Conclusions   108
4.8 POKEing the key buffer   120
4.9 Where next?   121

CHAPTER 5. MODIFYING THE HARDWARE   123

5.1 A few extra labels   123
5.2 The memory problem   124
5.3 Memory configuration   126
5.4 Opening it up   128
5.5 What's inside?   129
5.6 What else is there?   132
5.7 Adding the RAM   134
5.8 Customizing HP-28S and HP-28C menus   138
5.9 Subdirectories for the HP-28C   143

APPENDIX A. FURTHER SOURCES OF INFORMATION AND EQUIPMENT   155

APPENDIX B. PROBLEMS   161

Notes for users of the HP-28S and newer HP-28Cs.   169

APPENDIX C. THE STRUCTURE OF OBJECTS   171
         AND PROGRAMS

APPENDIX D. INTERNAL LAYOUT AND USE OF   177
         MACHINE LANGUAGE

Overall memory layout   177
The display RAM   179
HP-28S RAM and ROM   180
The Saturn CPU   181
HP-28C command name and address list   185
Notes   198

APPENDIX E. NEW VERSIONS OF THE HP-28   203

New and Changed Features of the HP-28S   204
SYSEVAL address on new versions   211

INDEX   217

PHOTOGRAPHS   225

Special HP-28 Keys and Symbols

Some HP-28 keys and symbols are difficult to represent using ordinary printer characters - this page explains how they are shown in the book.

The purple key is used to carry out the instructions written in purple above other keys. This is like a SHIFT key on a typewriter; it will be called SHIFT. For example, to select the statistics menu you press the purple key first, then the key with STAT in purple above it. Doing this will be written as just STAT.

The key with four arrows on it, to the right of the SHIFT key, is used to hide the menu labels which you normally see in the bottom row of the display. This lets the keys below the display act as "cursor" keys - they let you move the "cursor" symbol around the display according to the symbols printed above them, so the key is called the "cursor" key. It will sometimes be printed as <>. If you use the cursor key to see four lines of the display, then you can press it a second time to recover the current menu, unless you have done something else which deselects the current menu. A point to remember is that when the keys in the top row are used as cursor keys, they have special meanings if used with SHIFT. For example pressing the key marked > moves the cursor one place to the right, but pressing SHIFT and the > key moves you all the way to the right of the display. The cursor keys marked with the symbols < and > might be confused with the "greater than" and "less than" symbols, > and <, so I shall usually refer to the keys in the top row as INS, DEL, UP, DOWN, LEFT and RIGHT. When a menu is displayed I shall usually refer to the keys according to the label in the menu above them, just as if they were ordinary keys on the keyboard.

The left-arrow or back-arrow key deletes the character to the immediate left of the cursor. Calling this key DELETE might cause some confusion with the DEL cursor key; I shall usually call this the backarrow key or <-. The right-arrow key (used to create local variables, or a part of other command names) will usually be printed as ->.

The symbol for pi (SHIFT .) will just be written **pi**, symbols for "less than or equals", "greater than or equals", and "not equals" will be <=, >=, ≠. The curly d used as a differentiation symbol will be printed **d**, and the integral symbol will be INTEGRAL. SQRT will be used for the square root symbol. The symbols used to mark the beginning and end of a program will be printed as << and >>, the HP-28 design team call them "French quotes", since indeed they are often used instead of " by the French. The ' symbol will be called apostrophe or single quote. The alpha key, alpha lock and lower case (LC) will be called just that. If you press -> in Alpha Entry mode on an HP-28S then spaces will be put before and after it, for details see the end of Appendix B.

When a set of HP-28 keystrokes or a program is printed then keys which are pressed separately are printed with spaces between them. For example STO means "press the key marked STO", but X Y Z means "press X, then press Y and then Z." Numeric digits are printed without spaces between them, so 123 means "press 1, then 2 and then 3." If numbers have spaces between them then they really are separate numbers, for example 45 6 represents the two numbers 45 and 6. If an object does not all fit into the display, the HP-28 uses the ellipsis symbol ... to show that there is more to come at the right or left. When a piece of a program is printed in this book I use ellipsis symbols as well to show that it is only part of a program.

WARNING: Chapter Three of this book deals with the use of the SYSEVAL command. Use of the SYSEVAL command in these ways is not supported by Hewlett-Packard, making this a NOMAS (<u>N</u>ot <u>MA</u>nufacturer <u>S</u>upported) feature. As on all NOMAS features do <u>not</u> call Hewlett-Packard with questions about this. Also be aware that unpredictable behavior of the calculator is possible when using NOMAS features.

CHAPTER 1 – TIPS, KEYS AND MODES

This chapter deals with a few simple but important topics. First of all, here are three simple tips that should never be forgotten.

1.1 Read the manuals. The very first piece of advice is - read the manuals. The "Getting Started" manual introduces the HP-28 and many of its features, using very simple examples (if you need more examples they will be mentioned later). If you have already used another type of calculator which uses a "stack" then look at Appendix B in the Reference Manual; if you have used an "Algebraic Notation" calculator then read Appendix C of that manual. After that, read those parts of the Reference Manual that describe functions you know you will use. This is a very important first step - you most certainly cannot try to customize your HP-28 until you know how it works in the first place.

1.2 Do some examples. The Owner's Manual gives some examples to help you learn about the HP-28C, but these explain how it works, rather than how it can be used to solve problems. Hewlett-Packard now provide a set of examples with each HP-28C in addition to the two manuals, if your HP-28C did not have these then you can write to HP to ask for a set of examples. These examples are included in the HP-28S Owner's Manual. Very useful too are the Solution Books which HP have published for the HP-28C and HP-28S - these contain sets of related examples. In many cases these books show several different ways of solving the same problem - so you can choose a method that suits you best. This is a good way to customize your HP-28 - find out about the different ways to approach your kind of problems, and then pick the method you like best. At the same time you will, no doubt, come across some of the error and warning messages, and will come to realize that they are not enemies - they are actually trying to be helpful.

1.3 Keep notes. The HP-28 is about the same size as a pocket notebook. It is very helpful to carry such a notebook with your HP-

28 and to put down notes and ideas in it. While reading the manuals, while going through examples, and indeed while reading this book, you should make notes all the time. Later on, you can refer back to the notebook instead of carrying around a set of manuals. Once you start writing your own programs, you can copy them into the notebook as well; this is particularly important because the HP-28 does not provide any way of saving your programs, such as the card readers on the HP-65, HP-67, HP-97, HP-41, HP-75 and HP-71. The only mechanical way to save a program is to print it on the HP-82240A printer, but a small pocket notebook is much easier to carry with the HP-28 than is a printer. The HP-28C in particular does not have enough memory to store all your programs at the same time, so you should collect a set of programs which you can copy from your notebook to your HP-28C when you need them - and this method lets you use any HP-28 in the way you need it. One piece of advice - look after this notebook, put a return address in it or identify it in some way. If your HP-28 is stolen, you can buy another one, but it is much harder to replace the notes if they are stolen at the same time. It might not be wise to put your home address in the notebook though - a thief might steal your keys with it - use an office address or a telephone number.

* * *

Now for a few suggestions under the general heading of "keys".

1.4 Practice makes perfect. The HP-28 has <u>lots</u> of keys, and at first you might find it quite a nuisance looking for the right ones. It is a good idea to begin by using the HP-28 only as a simple calculator for a few days, with the left-hand keyboard folded underneath, so as to learn where the important keys are on the right-hand (numeric) keyboard. Then start using the lefthand keyboard too. Go through some examples (see 1.2 above) and you will soon begin to feel at home on the keyboards. If you really do find it difficult to look for keys or to remember command names then you can try using the CATALOG to look through the commands, and then to use FETCH in the CATALOG menu to fetch the command you want. After a few days you should find that you can remember the commands you use most and where the keys you need are, but you can always execute commands by spelling them out, by picking them from their own menu, by finding them in the CATALOG, or by writing a program which includes your command and assigning that to a key in the USER menu (see points 2.6 and 2.20). You can choose any one method or any combination of methods - and thus customize your use of the HP-28. In this book I assume you already know where most commands are, so I shall not always give detailed instructions on how to find a command.

1.5 Useful keys. You will soon learn that some keys are particularly useful. Clearly ON turns the calculator on, and combined with SHIFT turns it off - but at other times it acts as the ATTN key - it interrupts lengthy activities or programs and makes the calculator pay attention to the keyboard again. Sometimes ATTN interrupts an operation at once, for example pressing ATTN when a plot is complete clears the plot display at once; other operations will not stop at once. For example you can use ATTN to interrupt a printing command, but the command might not stop at once, because a print command can only be interrupted at certain places. Even then, the printer might carry on for quite some time, as it can store 200 characters and will carry on printing them even when the HP-28 stops sending characters to the printer. To stop the printer, turn it off and on again. The cursor key (<> next to SHIFT) can be used to hide the current menu and to activate the cursor keys instead, but remember that pressing this key a second time will bring back the menu, unless you have done something which cancels the current menu.

1.6 Useful key combinations. Note that you can use the cursor key (see above) to bring back the current menu at one keystroke, without the need for pressing SHIFT and a second key. If the second key is on the left-hand keyboard then this saves a considerable amount of finger moving.

There are many other ways to use single keys or key combinations which save effort compared to the normal method. One example is described in the manuals many times - you can carry out operations without using the final ENTER command. Thus:

35 * 67

can be carried with the following key strokes (I have used spaces to separate the keystrokes):

3 5 ENTER 6 7 ENTER *

but you can omit the second ENTER and do:

3 5 ENTER 6 7 *

This is because * automatically copies the command line to level 1 if that is required. Many other commands do the same. Another trick is to notice that a number can be doubled by:

ENTER +   or by 2 *

The first combination requires that you move a finger all the way from the top left to the bottom right of the numeric keyboard, so the second combination is quicker on the HP-28. In the same way, you can square a numeric or algebraic object which is in level 1 by doing:

ENTER *   or by   SHIFT +   or by   2 SHIFT *

The first of these three requires the least motion of your finger, but you might prefer one of the others, particularly if you touch-type on the HP-28 using more than one finger. Another trick: if you want to subtract the contents of level 1 from 17 then you can do:

17 SHIFT <- - (i.e.enter number, swap [SHIFT, backarrow] and subtract)

but it is quicker to do: 17 - CHS

All of the above suggestions except the first two are copied from similar suggestions for earlier HP calculators, in particular from suggestions made to me by Martin Lennaerts, and by Fleming Madsen and Steen Petersen of the Danish user club, while I was writing a book about the HP-41.

If you want to see further up the stack than is shown in the display then you can use SHIFT CHS (the VIEW^ command); but note two useful tricks. Firstly if you are using the bottom line of the display to show a menu, you can see level 4 by pressing the cursor key to show all four levels, and then bring back the menu by pressing <> again. The second is that after pressing VIEW^ several times you can bring back the original display by pressing ATTN; you do not have to use SHIFT EEX (VIEW down) several times.

One very useful key combination is SHIFT 7 (COMMAND) which returns the previous command line (unless you have disabled COMMAND). This lets you repeat a previous command or set of commands, and if you press SHIFT, 7 more than once you can bring back any of the last four command lines. You can then press ENTER to repeat the same command, or you can edit this command to execute a slightly different one.

The most common and natural way of executing a command line is to press the ENTER key, but you can use EVAL as well (unless you are in "alpha entry" mode, see point 1.13), and in some cases the EVAL key will be nearer your finger than ENTER, saving some effort by using EVAL.

A last suggestion here; it can be quicker to bring long command names to the command line by using a menu or the CATALOG than spelling out the command. For example Neville Joseph pointed out early on that spelling SYSEVAL uses seven key strokes, but SHIFT Q T followed by the PREV and FETCH menu keys takes only 5 key strokes. We shall see in 2.20 that it is even better to use a menu key.

* * *

Next some suggestions concerning the use of modes.

1.7 What is a mode? The word is used to mean several different things on the HP-28; the overall meaning is that a mode controls the way a result is evaluated, displayed, or printed. First of all, a mode is a setting which determines how the HP-28 behaves - for example it can do trigonometrical calculations in DEGrees mode or in RADians mode. Again, numbers can be displayed in STD, FIX, SCI or

ENG mode. This kind of mode is selected from a menu and stays set until it is specifically changed by another command. A second meaning of "mode" describes how keys affect the command line - you can have "insert" mode where new keystrokes are inserted into the command line, or "replace" mode where keystrokes replace (or "overwrite") characters in the command line with new characters. A third set of meanings for "mode" is "Entry Mode" - Immediate entry mode where objects are typed in and acted on at once, Algebraic entry mode which is initiated by the single quote key and which helps algebraic entry by adding the opening bracket after function names, and Alpha entry mode which enters command names into the command line and is therefore useful for keying in programs. Remember that the shape of the cursor shows the status of replace/insert mode and of the entry mode. In alpha mode you can also select a "lower case" mode; unfortunately there is no visual signal to tell you this mode is set. Users of the HP-41 and HP-71 will think of the HP-28 as being in "User" mode when the USER menu is displayed and the top row of keys responds according to variables created by the user. Other types of modes are described under the general heading "Modes" in chapter 1 of the Hewlett-Packard Reference Manual provided with your calculator. Many of the modes are controlled by the status of HP-28 flags and you can even use flags to invent new modes of your own.

1.8 Check your modes with PRMD. One of the most important ways in which you can customize the HP-28 to your own use is to set it to suitable modes. You can use the MODE menu to set and check many of the modes, but there are two quick ways find out what modes are set. Firstly, as mentioned above, the shape of the cursor shows you what keyboard entry mode is set. Secondly, you can use the PRMD (PRint MoDe) command from the PRINT menu or the MODE menu to show other modes. Either press SHIFT L NEXT and the third menu key (labelled PRMD), or simply type the letters P R M D and then press ENTER. The PRMD command is designed to let you print the HP-28 modes on the printer, but it also shows the modes in the display, so you can see them even if you have no printer. You can cancel the display by pressing any key; ATTN (the ON key) is usually best as it does not do anything else. If you have no printer, then you might find it annoying having to wait for the HP-28 while it tries to send all the information to the printer - point 1.17 suggests a way to speed this up.

1.9 Learn to use the modes. If you are doing your home finances on an HP-28 then you probably only want to display pounds and pence (or dollars and cents, or francs and centimes, and so on). Clearly it is useful to set the display to show whole numbers (pounds, dollars, etc.) followed by just two digits (pence, cents, etc.) and you can arrange for this to happen by setting the HP-28 to FIX 2 mode. You do this by typing 2 FIX and it may seem that this should be called 2 FIX mode, but on previous HP calculators it was called FIX 2 mode, and you can see that the PRMD display still uses this naming system. If you are a chemist doing titrations, you may prefer to display all results with a power of ten, and might choose SCI 4 mode, or if you are an engineer you might prefer ENG 6 mode. Whatever you choose, you are customizing your HP-28. If you are a non-British European you might prefer to use a comma to separate the fractional part of a number from its whole number part, and you can set this by changing the radix mode. By the way, the symbol which you choose <u>not</u> to act as a radix (the comma or dot) can be used as a separator instead of the space. For example, if you are using the dot as a radix then you can enter the complex number (1.0 , 2.0) by keying the characters (1 SPACE 2 ENTER or equally (1 , 2 ENTER. In many cases it is much easier to use the comma instead of going over to the left-hand keyboard just to press SPACE. Sometimes you will need to change from your preferred modes; point 2.12 will show how you can easily bring all modes back to your preferred setting with just one keystroke.

1.10 LAST, UNDO and COMMAND. These three commands are designed to help you recover from errors; they also let you repeat previous calculations, with changes if necessary. The HP-28 has only a small amount of memory to store information such as the stack, user variables, and the information required by LAST, UNDO and COMMAND - so there are modes which let you disable any combination of these commands, and save the space they would otherwise use. For instance UNDO has to save a complete copy of the stack as it was before you executed the most recent command - and if the stack has a lot of objects in it then this can use up valuable space in the memory. By disabling UNDO you can save all that space, but of course you lose the ability to recover from a mistake which altered the stack incorrectly.

1.11 A detailed look at LAST. The commands LAST, UNDO and COMMAND act in different ways; let us have a detailed look at LAST first (!). LAST recovers the stack objects used by the most recent command, even if this was ENTER (or DUP) in which case the object has just been duplicated on the stack. LAST will recover one, two or three objects - as many as were used by the most recent command; following DROP it will recover one object, following + it will recover two, and following an integration it will recover three. There are a few things to be careful with though. Some commands use no arguments (an object used by a command is called its "argument") and so do not change the value or values stored in LAST. Thus CLEAR will clear the whole stack but will leave LAST unchanged - of course you can use UNDO to get the stack back after CLEAR. The main purpose of LAST is to let you repeat calculations and correct mistakes - the HP-28 itself uses LAST to correct mistakes; if a mistake is found in a command and LAST is enabled then the HP-28 uses LAST to recover the original state of the stack, otherwise you might lose the incorrect object or objects.

Some commands can take more than three arguments, for example DROPN takes a number n from level 1 of the stack and drops n more objects from the stack. In this case, more than three objects might be lost, but LAST saves a maximum of three objects, so what happens? Commands such as DROPN are treated as "indirect" commands - the n values that were dropped were not referred to "directly" by the command. You can compare DROP2, which "directly" commands the dropping of 2 objects, to DROPN which "indirectly" commands the dropping of n objects, n being specified on the stack, not in the command itself. In commands like this the number n is treated as the argument and is saved in LAST, but the objects referred to "indirectly" are not saved - in the case of DROPN you can only recover them with UNDO. Other "indirect" commands which save only their "direct" argument in LAST are DUPN, PICK, ROLL and ROLLD - all these commands move objects in the stack but do not destroy the objects, so it is reasonable for them to save only the number n. DEPTH "uses" the objects in the stack in that it counts them, it but does not treat them as arguments, so it leaves the previous LAST value saved. Judging by this, SWAP might be expected to leave LAST unchanged, but actually it stores the objects from levels 1 and 2 in LAST, as they were before the SWAP command. Even more unexpected is the result of OVER, which brings a new copy of the object originally in level 2 into level 1 and lifts the stack; the effect of OVER is to store the objects that were in levels 1 and 2 in LAST, just like SWAP. ROT stores the objects that were in levels 1, 2 and 3 in LAST in their original order as might be predicted from the actions of OVER and SWAP.

Two other "indirect" commands which take a number n from level 1 and act on n more objects are ->ARRY and ->LIST. Both of these save n in LAST but all the other arguments can be recovered from the array or list created.

There is at least one other "indirect" command whose action may not be clear; it is PRVAR (Print Variable). All the other printer commands leave the stack and LAST unchanged, but PRVAR drops the name that was in level 1 and saves it in LAST - remember this when using a printer.

LAST can be enabled or disabled from the MODE menu, but also by the setting or clearing of flag 31. This means you can enable and disable LAST from a program, for example to save space at places which need a lot of memory.

1.12 More about UNDO and COMMAND. The UNDO command restores the whole stack as it was before the previous command. If that previous command was the name of a program then the UNDO command restores the stack as it was before the program started. The main use of UNDO is to get back the whole stack as it originally was before a command if you notice that you have used the wrong command. Remember that using UNDO destroys the present contents of the stack, unlike LAST which brings back the latest arguments and pushes them onto the stack, leaving everything else as it was. The UNDO command does not cancel itself - so if you decide that you had not meant to use it then you cannot use UNDO again to bring back the stack as it was before.

COMMAND is the most powerful of the three "correction" commands - it brings back to the command line the most recent contents of the command line, and if you repeat it then it brings back the second most recent command line, then the third, then the fourth - after which it goes back to the most recent command line again. Executing COMMAND recovers the command line; it cannot be used to recover a command that was executed directly by pressing a key. For example if you press the DROP key in direct execution mode then you cannot recover the DROP command by using COMMAND. On the other hand, if you press DROP in alpha entry mode, or spell out the word DROP, and press ENTER or EVAL then you will be able to bring DROP back to the command line with COMMAND. The extra power of COMMAND lies in the fact that you can edit any command line brought back by it. For example you can type in the command line:

$$\text{'(SIN(X)+3)^2}$$

and press EVAL to evaluate this expression. Then you can use COMMAND to bring back the expression and edit it to change the power from 2 to 3, and evaluate the new expression, and you can repeat this as many times as necessary. Executing COMMAND lets you evaluate the same formula with different values, or evaluate a set of similar formulae - it provides an alternative to writing and storing a program.

Neither UNDO nor COMMAND can be enabled or disabled from within a program by normal means, but point 3.7 will show how SYSEVAL provides a way around this limitation. In any case, LAST, UNDO and COMMAND provide a powerful set of commands that you can use to control the HP-28 in ways that suit you, so their use can help you customize your HP-28.

1.13 A look at the command line. The example above shows how the command line can be recovered and edited to make new commands. Let us have a more detailed look at the command line and how it is affected by entry modes.

In the normal "immediate entry" mode you can type in real numbers, complex numbers, arrays and other objects - all these go into the command line. It is only when you press ENTER that these objects are put into level 1 of the stack. On previous HP calculators you could normally only type numbers from the keyboard directly into the bottom level of the stack; there was no intermediate step such as the command line. One clear advantage of the command line is that it can be used to edit an object that is in level 1. Thus you might type in a long number, press ENTER, then realize the number has the last digit wrong. On the HP-28, you can press EDIT, correct the last digit, then press ENTER to put the number back on the stack. If you put in a number, then press something such as + or SIN, then realize the number was wrong, you can use LAST or UNDO, then EDIT to correct the number, then repeat the command. All this is much easier than on previous HP calculators - if a number was wrong you usually had to delete it completely with CLX, then start again. If the number at the bottom of the stack was the result of a calculation then again it was difficult to change it; say you want to check the result of a trig expression if you evaluate it for pi, then want to check it again with the last digit of pi changed. On the HP-28 you can press **pi**, then ->NUM, then EDIT and change the last digit - this is much easier than on a calculator which shows only one level of the stack and does not let you edit numbers. One more point - if you want to edit any other stack level, you can VISIT it or recall it to level 1 with PICK, then edit it. Examples of editing are given in the manuals and in the solution books.

In "immediate entry" mode, if you press any key except those used to create objects, that key will carry out its command or function.

This usually stops entry of the command line, so after using immediate entry mode you can only use COMMAND to edit data objects. If you want to enter and edit an algebraic object or a set of commands in the command line, then you need to use "algebraic entry" mode or "alpha entry" mode. In algebraic entry mode you can enter numbers and objects, as in immediate entry mode, but pressing a function key (SIN, +, TANH and so on) puts the function name in the command line, and if the function needs an argument then its name is followed by a bracket, for example SIN(or TANH(. This lets you create an algebraic expression in the command line, as in the previous example. Such an expression can be used, recalled by COMMAND, then edited and used again.

In "alpha entry" mode, objects, functions, and commands as well are all put in the command line. Say you want to multiply two numbers together and print the result. You could do:

press ALPHA (bottom right key of alpha keyboard),
press 35, then SPACE
press 67, then SPACE, then *
press PRINT, then the menu key labelled PR1
press DROP

The command line now has all the instructions required to calculate 35*67, then print the result on the printer, then drop the result off the stack.

Now you can press ENTER to leave alpha entry mode and carry out all the instructions in the command line. To repeat the calculation and printing, you can use COMMAND to bring back the whole command line, then use SHIFT < to go back to the beginning of the line, and (for example) type 49 over the 35 - now you can press ENTER again, and the HP-28 will print the result of 49*67. Then you can repeat the whole trick again for another number. All this is much easier than pressing all the keys each time for each calculation. You could do this on earlier HP calculators by writing a program, and you can do the same on the HP-28 too, but it can be much quicker to use the command line to repeat one particular kind of operation a few times, instead of writing and storing a program.

In summary, "immediate entry" mode lets you use the HP-28 like one of the earlier HP calculators - numbers are entered into the stack (from the command line) and functions are carried out at once. "Algebraic entry" mode lets you use the HP-28 like an algebraic calculator - you type an algebraic expression into the command line, then evaluate it by pressing ENTER or EVAL. "Alpha entry" mode is like a BASIC computer where you can type in a line of commands, and if the line does not have a line number then pressing ENTER makes the computer carry out the commands in the line. Just by choosing the appropriate entry mode you can customize your HP-28 to work in any one of these three ways.

1.14 About ENTER. Once you have typed in a command line, you press the ENTER key to copy the line to level 1, or to carry out the commands in the line. It is worth knowing some more details about the command line and ENTER. While you are putting objects and commands into the command line, they are held there as a string of characters. For example the command DUP is held in the command line as the letters D U P , not as a command. In the same way, the number 12.75 is held in the command line as 1 2 . 7 5 , not as a number. When you press ENTER, the HP-28 goes through the command line and turns everything into objects or commands, which are stored in the HP-28 in quite a different way, as a program. If there are no mistakes, the HP-28 carries out the program, and you just see that the command line has been worked out for you.

While it translates the command line, the HP-28 checks for simple errors, such as spelling mistakes which result in unrecognized commands. If any such error is found, it is highlighted by the cursor for you to correct. This means that the command line is still in the HP-28 while it is being translated. If you type in a very long command line, then a lot of memory is needed to hold the whole line and also the whole program it is being translated to. In fact, a very long command line might cause an HP-28C to run out of memory. That is one reason why it is safer to use the HP-28C with short programs and command lines, not long ones. If you copy a long command line to level 1, say a complicated algebraic expression, then try to EDIT it, you will need room for the original expression, for the command line in which it is being edited, for the UNDO copy and the COMMAND stack copy, and for the new translation. It is clear that with five versions of the expression, but 1500 bytes available at most, an HP-28C can easily run out of memory in such a case; an HP-28S should have no trouble.

Each character in the HP-28 is represented by a "byte" - a number between 0 and 255. The number corresponding to each character is given in a table in the STRING section of the HP-28 Reference manual. The numbers from 32 to 126 are standard codes used by very many computers; they are called ASCII (American Standard Code for Information Interchange), the others are an extension of ASCII, called ROMAN 8. The end of the command line is marked by a null byte - a special character with a numeric value of zero. When you are editing the command line in replace mode, the null byte helps the HP-28 tell where the end of the command line comes, so you will not accidentally start editing information past the end of the command line. This is why you are prevented from editing a text line which contains character zero - the HP-28 would not be able to tell a character zero in the middle of the line from the character marking the end of the line.

If the command line contains only a data object, then it is translated into a program which simply puts that object on the stack, otherwise it is translated into a set of objects, an algebraic expression, or a whole collection of objects and commands. All these are carried out, or put on the stack, depending on their nature. The symbol << has a special meaning. If it appears in a command line then the instructions after this symbol are translated into a program which is put onto the stack, instead of being carried out at once. This is the way in which you can write your own programs and store them, as will be described in the next chapter.

Pressing ENTER at any time when there is no command line makes the HP-28 put a copy of the object in level 1 into level 2 of the stack and lift the rest of the stack.   This is precisely the way ENTER worked on earlier HP calculators, and it was sensible to retain it on the HP-28 - in this case ENTER behaves like DUP.   However pressing ENTER if the command line does contain an object causes that object to be moved from the command line to stack level 1. Pressing ENTER a second time now will copy the object in level 1 into level 2, making a second copy.   This is <u>not</u> the same as happened on previous HP calculators - typing a number into a calculator and pressing ENTER once made two copies of the number in the stack, and pressing ENTER twice made three copies.   When using ENTER on the HP-28, you must remember that there is a command line below the first stack level.   My thanks to Colin Crowther for pointing out this pitfall.

1.15 Other modes. Many modes are controlled by user flags 31 to 64 as listed in the table of "Reserved User Flags" in Chapter 1 of the Reference Manual. A full understanding of these flags and the modes they control lets you use them to set up the HP-28 to work just as you need - to "customize" it.   Unfortunately the explanations in the table are sometimes too brief to be helpful, for example flag 45 is described as "Level 1 display" - in fact it controls whether or not you have a multiline display of programs, lists, and two-dimensional arrays in level 1.   It can be very useful to write out a list of these flags and what they do, and to carry it around, either in your pocket notebook, or on a label glued to the HP-28.   Remember that you can set or clear all these flags, so any mode controlled by them can be controlled from within a program.

1.16 Create your own modes.   Flags 31 to 64 all have special meanings, but you can use flags 1 to 30 in a very similar way - to create your own modes.   For example you might want to calculate temperatures in degrees Celsius or Fahrenheit - you could choose to set flag 5 when working in Celsius and clear flag 5 when working in Fahrenheit.   Then you could write programs which check this flag and make decisions accordingly, and you could use the built-in units system to convert from one type of degrees to another as and when necessary. Clearly this is a way to customize your HP-28 by creating new types of modes.

1.17 Using the printer control flags. Flags 33 and 52 are normally used to control the printer, but they can be used to speed up the PRMD display as well. If you set flags 52 and 33 then information is sent to the printer more quickly and without carriage returns between lines. This speeds up the sending of the mode information to the printer by the PRMD command, which might be a good thing if you are using PRMD without a printer - see point 1.8 above.

CHAPTER 2 - VARIABLES, PROGRAMS & MENUS

The main aim of this chapter is to show how you can write programs to make the HP-28 do exactly those things that you want, but I begin with a related topic - constants and variables. If you already know about programming the HP-28, look quickly through this chapter; there are some useful tips in it.

2.1 Simple constants. The HP-28 provides some commands which produce a simple constant. For example pressing SHIFT . generates the constant pi. Pi is common on scientific calculators, but the HP-28 also provides the constants e, i, MINR and MAXR. The point about pi and e, i, MINR, MAXR is that they are recognized as special symbols which can be replaced by a numeric value when you wish.

The HP-28 lets you create your own symbols and constants too. If you want to differentiate SIN(A) without knowing what the value of A is, then the HP-28 lets you do that by means of its symbolic differentiation ability - in this case A is a symbol. You can also create a symbol whose value you do know, and use the symbol name instead of having to type in its numeric value during calculations. Say you are doing some calculations involving G, the universal gravitational constant. The value of G in SI units is 6.670E-11 m^3*kg^-1*s^-2 so you can create a symbol called G and give it this value by doing:

     6.67 EEX 11 CHS G STO

If you press the USER key to display the USER menu you will see the letter G above the top left-hand key of the right-hand keyboard. You have created a variable called G. If you had already created a variable called G then it might be somewhere else in the user menu. (HP-28S owners should be careful which subdirectory G is in; I shall discuss HP-28S subdirectories in Chapter 5, elsewhere I shall assume everything is in the HOME directory.)   You can now use G in very much the same way as you can use the command pi. Say you want to calculate:

$$\frac{G*5.976E24}{6.3782E6^2}$$

You can do the following:

press the ' key
press the menu key labelled G
enter the rest of the expression: *5.976EEX24/6.3782EEX6^2

Now you can press ENTER to put the expression on the stack or EVAL to evaluate its numeric value. You can carry on using G like this in other expressions much like pi or e or any other constant provided by the HP-28. You have created a new constant which you can use like the others, and by creating such constants you are adding to the commands available on your HP-28, so you are customizing it.

2.2 Simple variables. At some time you might discover that the universal gravitational constant has been determined more accurately, so you might want to change the numeric value of G. You can do this very easily by simply typing in the new value then typing in 'G and then pressing STO. (Note that once G has been created you cannot store new values unless you put a quote in front of the name G, to show it is a name.) On the other hand, you certainly can not change the values of pi or e stored in the HP-28. For this reason, G and any other object created in the same way on an HP-28 is called a "variable" - you can vary its value.

In the case of G, you would not be likely to want to change the numeric value often, but you can create variables whose values change all the time. For example to use the HP-28 to solve quadratic equations you might create variables X1 and X2 which will contain the roots of the quadratic equation. If the quadratic has real roots then X1 and X2 will contain real numbers, if the roots are complex, then X1 and X2 will contain complex numbers. The HP-28 will take care of details like this and will store whatever you wish in the variables. You can then solve another quadratic, and have

its roots in X1 and X2, or you can use X1 and X2 just like pi or G
to provide commands which will let you use these numbers in further
calculations.

Variables like X1 and X2 can store a real number or a complex
number; and they can store more complicated objects too - vectors,
matrices, strings and so on. Anything that you can put on the stack
by typing it in from the keyboard or by creating it some other way
can be stored in a variable. Say you want a unit matrix of
dimension 2*2 then you can do the following:

[[1 , 0 [0 , 1 ENTER U2 STO

This creates a variable called U2 which contains the 2*2 unit
matrix. Whenever you need such a matrix in future, you can bring it
to level 1 of the stack just by pressing USER and the key labelled
U2. Note that you do not need to press] to separate the rows of a
matrix - the HP-28 only allows one- and two-dimensional matrices, so
a third or subsequent [is recognized as closing one row and opening
the next.

2.3 Commands or variables? A command is any programmable HP-28
operation. For example SWAP makes the HP-28 swap the objects in
levels 1 and 2, SIN works out the sine of the object in level 1, and
DRAW draws a plot of the equation stored in EQ. If we look at pi or
e or MAXR again, we can see that they are all commands too; they are
a special type of command which puts an object into level 1 of the
stack. You can get them by spelling them out, pressing a single
keyboard key, or selecting a menu and pressing a key on that menu;
in each case the HP-28 recognizes pi, e or MAXR because these names
are built into the HP-28, and it carries out these commands.

After you create a variable such as G or X1 and X2 described in
points 2.1 and 2.2 above, you can fetch that value by spelling out
the name of the variable, or by pressing a menu key which
corresponds to the variable's name. This is just the same as
carrying out a command such as pi or MAXR. The main difference
between a command such as pi and a variable such as G is that the
command is built into the HP-28, and the variable is created by you,

the user.   In other words, a variable is really a new command created by the user, and added to the list of commands built into the HP-28.

Simple variables such as G or X1 and X2 just put a new number into stack level 1, much the same as the simple commands pi or MAXR. Most commands do something more complicated, and variables can do more complicated jobs too.   One example: to put a 2*2 unit matrix in level 1 of the stack you can use the command IDN by doing:

2 IDN ENTER

Equally well you can press USER and the key labelled U2 to bring back the 2*2 unit matrix which you had stored at the end of point 2.2. Once again we see that a variable is doing the same job as a command.   The USER menu is really there to let the user create his or her own new commands, and use them just like commands built into the HP-28; it is there to let you customize the HP-28 by adding new commands that you need.

2.4 Variables and programs. So far we have only stored numbers (real or complex) and a matrix into variables.   If you have read the manuals and used your HP-28 before reading this book then you know that other objects, including programs, can be stored in variables. This makes good sense - if variables are user-written commands then you might need to write commands which do more than put an object onto the stack.   Here is a very simple example: you have probably noticed that you often use the pair of commands SWAP DROP to remove an object from level 2 of the stack.   It can be useful to have a command which does this at the pressing of a single key.   This command can be created by writing a short program as follows:

press << SWAP DROP
press ENTER - the program is copied to level 1 of the stack and >> is added
type in a name for this command, say NIP, then press STO
press USER and you will see the new variable NIP in the menu

To try out this command, press 1 ENTER 2 ENTER and then press the key labelled NIP and see that the 1 has been removed from level 2. NIP is a new command which "nips" the object out of level 2. This HP-28 command was suggested to me by Jean-Daniel Dodin. NIP and TUCK (<< SWAP OVER >>) are standard words in the Laxen/Perry F83 implementation of FORTH.

You might be surprised that the variable G brings a number to the stack, but NIP does not bring the program to level 1 of the stack - it executes the program stored in NIP. The confusion is partly due to the name "variable" - in fact G and NIP are both "commands" - G is a command which puts a number on the stack, NIP is a command which carries out SWAP DROP. Both commands have been created by you, the user, and both are available on the USER menu. Anything stored by the user can be changed later; you can put a different number into G, you can put a different program in NIP, or you could put a matrix into NIP and a string of letters into G - you can vary their contents, so they are called "variables" as on most computers and in most programming languages. Nevertheless, it is useful to think of them as user-written commands.

If you do want to bring a program back to the stack, you can press ', then the program name (on the USER menu), then RCL (SHIFT STO). If you want to change the program without bringing it back to the stack, you can do the same, but use VISIT instead of RCL.

2.5 COMMAND and programs. In the previous chapter I showed how you can use a set of commands repeatedly by typing them into the command line once, then bringing them back by use of COMMAND. From the point above you can see that a set of commands can also be stored in a variable for repeated use. Once again, the HP-28 provides more than one way of doing something - you can pick the method which suits you best. Of the two, a program is easier to execute - you just press a single key, and of course a program is stored permanently. A command line can be edited more easily, and it does not require any special effort to save it - but if you carry out more than three other operations which use the command line then the command line you want can no longer be recovered with COMMAND. A program has one other advantage - its name can be used as a command in other programs. Say you need a command to add together the numbers in levels 1 and 2, then to put the number that was originally in level 1 back into level 1. You could do this with the following simple program:

<< + LAST SWAP DROP >>

As we already have the program NIP which does SWAP DROP , we can simplify the above to do:

<< + LAST NIP >>

How does this work? Say you have a stack set up as below:

        3:    'A*G/17.93'
        2:        1.57981
        1:        -1.2138

the addition changes the stack to:

        2:    'A*G/17.93'
        1:        .36601

LAST changes it to:

        4:    'A*G/17.93'
        3:        .36601
        2:        1.57981
        1:        -1.2138

NIP nips out the object in level 2, leaving the result of the addition in level 2 and the original contents of level 1 still there:

        3:    'A*G/17.93'
        2:        .36601
        1:        -1.2138

You could write the second of the above programs by doing:

a. press   <<   (Note that this   automatically puts the HP-28 into alpha entry mode. At other times you have to do that yourself.)
b. press + , then press LAST
c. press NIP   This is a USER   menu key, since we just wrote NIP above.

d. press ENTER

e. store the new program by pressing A D D L   STO

The new program is stored in a variable called ADDL. Is it any use?
Well, it replicates what would happen on older HP calculators if you
pressed + and LASTX, so it helps if you are translating HP-41
programs for the HP-28.

2.6 Simple programs. NIP is a very short program - we can write much
longer ones, but first let us look at some more short programs. NIP
has only two commands in it; it can sometimes be useful to write
programs with just one step. An example would be if you were doing
calculations on real numbers, with the USER menu displayed, but
sometimes needed to get the integer part of a number. You can get
the integer part of the number in level 1 by pressing EDIT, and
deleting the fractional part. You could also select the REAL menu,
then press NEXT twice, or PREV twice, then press the menu key
labelled IP, then press USER to get back to the user menu. Both
methods take a lot of key pushing and it is much quicker to press I
then P then ENTER, which carries out the IP command in just three
keystrokes. Even so, you have to go to the left hand keyboard to do
this, which is awkward, particularly if you have it folded under the
right hand keyboard. The simplest trick is to write a program which
contains just the one command IP, and to put this program into a
variable on the USER menu:

a. press << , then press I and then P
b. press ENTER to create the program << IP >>
c. type in a name for the program (see below), then press STO

Now you will be able to carry out IP by pressing just one key,
without leaving the USER menu and without using the left hand
keyboard.

One problem is that you cannot call this program IP, as that is
already the name of the built-in IP command. You could use some
similar name, say INTP (INTeger Part); a neater trick is to use the

same name, IP, but put a lower case letter in the name. Press I then LC (Lower Case mode selection key) and P then STO. You will have given the program the name 'Ip'; as the USER menu does not show lower case letters, it will show a key labelled IP. Now you have a key labelled IP, which carries out the IP command, but available from the USER menu. Press ' and the key to check what the program name really is - you will see 'Ip in the command line - you will need to use this name if you want to edit the program or PURGE it. It is better not to use lower case letters alone in names like this, see the end of point 2.14.

Naturally the same tricks allow other commands to be used directly from the USER menu. One problem is that you can have no more than six variables displayed at a time - to get more you will need to use NEXT or PREV, or re-order them with ORDER. This will be described under point 2.18.

Using lower case letters for a replacement command name can be helpful at other times. Imagine you are picking objects out of a list. GET will pick an object out of a list in level 2, but will lose the list. GETI will save the list, but will add 1 to the index. You might want to write your own version of GETI, to pick out the object at the place given by the index, without changing the index. You could write the program:

<< GETI SWAP 1 - SWAP >>

then store it with the name Geti, using lower case e t i (type the letter G as usual, then press LC and E T I). Now you would have your own GETI, customized to suit your needs. To make sure that nothing goes wrong when the index is at the end of the list, you could write a slightly longer version:

<< -> I << I GETI NIP I SWAP >> >>

using the program NIP which was introduced earlier, or using SWAP DROP in its place if you prefer. In this version the index is stored in the local variable I, and restored from it, so that you will not produce a 0 by subtracting 1 from the updated index when it goes past the end of the list and is reset to 1. (Local variables are described in point 2.7 which comes next.) This version of GETI is designed to work with lists - it will not work with two-dimensional arrays; you could write a version to do that too.

These two examples should show you that even very short programs can be used in various ways to customize your HP-28.

2.7 Longer programs. In any but the shortest programs you are likely to need to make tests and carry out different sets of commands depending on the results, or to need to repeat a set of commands. Details are given in the Reference Manual under the titles - Programs, Program Branch, Program Control and Program Test. It is worth studying all these sections, here I shall give just one example of how a program can be developed to use some of these features.

Say you want a new command to calculate the SINC function of the object in level 1. SINC is defined as:

$$SINC(X) = SIN(X)/X$$

A simple program to calculate SINC would be:

<< SIN LAST / >>

Actually, LAST might be disabled, so it would be better to use DUP to make a second copy of the object in level 1.

Another problem is that level 1 might contain a zero! In this case the division will give an error. The value of SINC(X) approaches 1 as X tends to zero, and it is exactly 1 when X is zero, but the program above would not work this out. Let us rewrite the program to deal with both problems:

<< DUP IF 0 == THEN DROP 1
ELSE DUP SIN SWAP / END >>

Now we have duplicated the object in level 1 and checked whether it is equal to zero. 0 == is a test which will give the result 1 if the object is equal to zero, and 0 if it is not. THEN will check the result of this test, if the result is any number except 0 then the test was true, and the commands after THEN will be carried out.

If the result is 0, then the test was false, and the commands between ELSE and END will be carried out, or nothing will be done if there is no ELSE. In this program the commands after THEN are DROP 1 which removes the remaining copy of the value and puts in the result 1. (You could replace these two commands with the one command FACT which converts a zero into a 1.) If the value is not zero, then the test result will be zero, which means "not true", so the commands between ELSE and END will calculate SINC using the normal formula (and making two copies of the value, so LAST does not have to be relied on).

Even this is not perfect - we should really check flag 60 first to see if the HP-28 is in radians mode, since SINC works correctly in radians mode. It is up to you whether you include such a test or leave it to the user to check the angle mode. The above program is already rather complicated by the use of DUP and DROP, so we won't worry about that here.

This program is a little complicated - it might be difficult to follow what is happening on the stack. One way to check this is to write out what is in the stack after each step; you can do this on a scrap of paper or you can produce a properly designed "stack analysis form" on which you write each step and what it does to the stack. It can be quite important to do this, otherwise you might leave spare copies of some object on the stack; and the stack can quickly fill up the whole memory of an HP-28C. One of the advantages of the HP-28 over previous calculators is that up to four levels of the stack can be seen, so it is much easier to follow what is happening to the stack during a calculation. See point 2.9 as well.

We could make the program easier to understand if we copied the object from level 1 into a "local variable". If we begin the program with:

-> X

then the HP-28 takes the object from level 1 and puts it in a variable X. Within the program, we can use X to mean "the object that was in level 1", but when the program ends X will vanish. Now we can rewrite the above:

$$<< \; -> \; X \; << \; IF \; X \; 0 \; == \; THEN \; 1$$
$$ELSE \; X \; SIN \; X \; / \; END \; >> \; >>$$

This is no shorter than the previous version, but it is much easier to understand. Here X is a "local variable" - it is only used locally, in this program, and will not be available after the program has finished. See point 2.14 for some tricks with local variables.

The program could be rewritten again to use IFTE instead of IF, THEN, ELSE and END:

$$<< \; -> \; X \; << \; X \; 0 \; == \; 1 \; << \; X \; SIN \; X \; / \; >> \; IFTE \; >> \; >>$$

In this version, we put three objects on the stack; first the result of the test X 0 == (if the test is true then a one is left on the stack, otherwise a zero). Next comes a 1 (this will be the answer if the test is true), and thirdly comes the program to work out SINC if the test is not true. IFTE uses all three objects. If the result of the test (in level 3) is not a zero then the object in level 2 is evaluated and left as the result, if the result is false (zero), then the object in level 1 is evaluated and left as the result.

Now for a trick to save a few steps. Note that we can invert the test ($\neq$ instead of ==) and invert the two possible results, getting the same answer. The test would become:

$$X \; 0 \; \neq$$

but this simply puts a zero (false result) on the stack if X is zero, and puts a one (true result) on the stack if X is not zero. We could get exactly the same result by just leaving X itself on the stack! After all, zero means false, non-zero means true. So the program can be rewritten one more time:

$$<< \; -> \; X \; << \; X \; << \; X \; SIN \; X \; / \; >> \; 1 \; IFTE \; >> \; >>$$

This is shorter than the earlier versions, but it is still clear what it does if you remember that X itself can be used as the result of a true/false test. There is still a problem (isn't there always?) - if the object in level 1 is not a number but a name or an expression then this version of the program will not work. We could try to rewrite the program completely to deal with symbolic values, we could use a user-defined function (see next point), we could just force X to turn into a number if possible by using ->NUM:

   << -> X << X ->NUM << X SIN X / >> 1 IFTE >> >>

or we could just say "this is a program to calculate SINC of the object in level 1 if that object is a number".

Let's do the last - we have done about enough with one program; it has shown how a simple idea needs to be expanded, and then how the resulting program can be made simpler again, but that there may still be problems. You could, if you wish, try writing shorter programs to do the same calculation, but they would probably not be as clear. One possible trick is to notice that the result of the test X == 0 is 1 if X is zero, and 1 is the value that SINC takes if X is zero.

2.8 Algebraic expressions. We have seen how variables can be used to create new commands which put objects on the stack, or which are combinations of other commands. Variables can be used to store other objects too, including algebraic expressions. For example you could STO '3*SIN(X)' in a variable called SIN3, then recall this to level 1 by pressing the key labelled SIN3.

You can do the same with the program << SIN 3 * >> but the algebraic expression is clearer than the program. Another advantage of algebraic expressions is that they let us write our own "functions" on an HP-28C: the programs shown above work out SINC of the object in level 1, but they can not be used in algebraic expressions. We could not use them on an HP-28C in an expression such as:

'3*LOG(SINC(X))'

because the HP-28C only knows that SINC is a variable, not that it works like an algebraic function. By rewriting the last program as an algebraic though, we can turn SINC into a "user-defined function"

(UDF) which the HP-28C will recognize in algebraic expressions:

    << -> X 'IFTE(X, SIN(X)/X, 1)' >> ' S I N C STO

This new program uses the algebraic form of IFTE, with its three arguments (test, true-action, false-action) all written in algebraic form. When the program is evaluated, it thus returns an algebraic expression, so in effect the variable SINC contains an algebraic expression. Now we could use this latest version of SINC in an expression such as '3*LOG(SINC(X))' and the HP-28C would evaluate this with no trouble, so long as X is a number or can be evaluated to a number. SINC is not followed by a bracket when you press its menu key in algebraic entry mode; otherwise it works in the same way as a function built into the HP-28C. You can even define a derivative for it!

The programs written in the previous point will fail if you try using them to calculate SINC of a variable which has not been given a value. The user-defined function will not fail; it is an algebraic expression and can deal with symbolic values. However, try calculating SINC(ZZ); assuming you do not have a variable called ZZ you will see SINC(ZZ) evaluates to the expression:

    'IFTE(ZZ,SIN(X)/X,1)'

The first X is replaced by ZZ, but ZZ has no value so the rest of IFTE cannot be evaluated; it is left as a symbolic expression. The result is thus an algebraic expression; it is symbolically correct but it will not work out the correct answer if ZZ is given a numeric value later. This is because the second argument of IFTE was left as SIN(X)/X and X is an undefined local name. That could be considered a shortcoming of the HP-28 - it would be nice if all the Xs could be replaced by ZZ at the same time. Even so, the user-defined function has a clear advantage over any program, since it does give an algebraic expression, not an error message.

This shows one way in which it can be very useful to create variables that contain algebraic expressions - you can create your own mathematical functions, in other words, once again, you can customize your HP-28.

NOTE: on an HP-28S you <u>can</u> use programs in algebraic expressions; even if SINC is a program an HP-28S recognizes SINC(X) as a user defined function in '3*LOG(SINC(X))'. This gives extra versatility to UDFs on an HP-28S, since commands can be used in programs, but not in algebraic expressions.

2.9 Writing and testing programs. Up till now I have been describing only programs which behave like additional HP-28 commands. Clearly you can write other sorts of program which do much more than a single command. You could write a program which asks for two numbers, integrates a function between them, prints the result and an error estimate, then asks for another pair of numbers - this would be similar to the integrate function, but much more "user-friendly" - it would be a true program, not just a command. The HP-28 Example Books give examples of such programs, here I shall just make some suggestions concerning program writing and testing.

A clear rule is that programs should be short. If you need a long program, write it in several pieces. The user-friendly program to integrate between two limits could be split into three parts: part A <u>a</u>sks for two numbers, B does the <u>b</u>asic integration, and C <u>c</u>opies the results to the printer. You could write three sub-programs called A, B and C to do these three things, (on an HP-28S you could put them in a subdirectory) then a main program to put all three parts together . This main program could simply be:

<< A B C >>

or it could include a WHILE...REPEAT command to keep repeating the three parts until some condition is met that finishes the set of values; you could for instance test that the upper and lower limits are both zero.

One reason for doing this on an HP-28C is that it has only a small amount of memory available for writing and storing programs. While a program is being written or edited, you might have as many as five copies of it in the memory. It takes much less memory to keep five copies of a short program than five copies of a long one. If you split a long job into several small pieces then you will only be editing one piece at a time, using less memory, so you will be less likely to get the dreaded "Out of Memory" warning. The only problem is that at the end you use a little more memory for all the small subprograms plus the main program than you would for just one program. It would be very nice if the + command could be used to add together several small programs into one large program!

Another reason for writing small programs is that they are much easier to test. The HP-28 does not provide step numbers for programs; if a program with 114 steps goes wrong somewhere then it is very difficult to find which of the 114 commands is the one in error! When an HP-28 program goes wrong, you just get a BEEP and an error message, with no indication of where the program went wrong (HP-28S messages help somewhat by giving the name of the command that found the error). You might be able to use the contents of the stack to work out what was happening, but this is not always possible. It is much easier to split a program of about 100 steps into four or five subprograms of about 20 steps each. Then you can test each subprogram separately, before trying to use them all together.

If you do find a problem in a program or subprogram, a <u>very</u> useful trick is to put HALT at the beginning of the program. When you press the key to run the program, it will stop at once, with the suspended program annunciator turned on. Now you can select the Program Control menu (SHIFT M), then press the SST (Single STep) menu key repeatedly to see the program carried out one step at a time. When you reach the command which detects an error, you will hear a BEEP and see a message. If you wish, you can change the stack or any variables, then carry on with the program by using SST. Alternatively, once you have corrected the problem, you can press CONT (SHIFT 1) to let the program continue running. If you decide to correct the program, or to stop it running, press the menu key labelled KILL to stop the program, this will turn off the suspended program annunciator, and will release all the space reserved for the running program. KILL is probably better than ABORT, since it stops all other suspended programs, which might have been waiting to use the results of this program. (As the design team leader admits, the HP-28 has a pretty violent set of commands, what with KILL, ABORT, PURGE, not to mention terms that are more ambivalent, such as CROSS, DROP, or HEX.)

Remember that when you stop a program with HALT and then SST through it, you will only SST through the program you have HALTed. A subprogram called from inside the HALTed program will be carried out as a single step, and if the HALTed subprogram returns control to a program which started it, then that program will carry on running. To follow through several programs you will need a HALT in each one. If you want to trace through a long program or set of programs you can use several other methods. One trick is to DISP something (a number or a message) every few steps, so you can see how your program is doing. Another is to make a different BEEP every few steps, so the sound of the program tells you how you are progressing. Yet another method is to set the printer mode to TRACE and to watch the results printed out by the program as it works through its task. Unfortunately this can use up an awful lot of paper.

2.10 Some space saving tips. If you are writing a long program and despite all your attempts you run out of memory, then you will have to split it up into even smaller pieces, or make it shorter in some other way, or free some memory. Clearing the stack and PURGEing some user variables can help; if that is not enough then disable LAST and UNDO. Do not disable COMMAND until you really have to; if you run out of memory when you press ENTER after entering a program, then COMMAND will let you recover the program if it is not disabled, otherwise you will lose everything you have done.

If all else fails, you will have to find a shorter way to write the program (or pay to get an HP-28 with more memory). Use shorter names for variables, make messages and other text strings shorter. Note that the numbers -9 to -1, 0 and 1 to 9 take up two and a half bytes each, as do commands, whereas other real numbers take up 16 bytes. Thus 3 INV takes only five bytes, whereas 0.333333 takes 16 - savings can often be made in this way. Remember that algebraic expressions generally use more memory than equivalent stack notation (RPN) expressions, and arrays take less memory and are faster to use than equivalent lists.

You might also find that some HP-28 commands you do not use much could replace several steps or even a whole program. One such command is RSD. RSD is designed to compute the residual array B - AZ where B is an array in level 3 of the stack, A is a matrix in level 2, and Z is an array in level 1. Clearly RSD can be used to calculate B - AZ whenever you are using arrays, not just when you need a residual. Another example I have already given (in point 2.7) is using FACT to replace a zero with a one.

2.11 Subprograms and routines. The use of subprograms to build up larger programs has already been mentioned. Sometimes you will find that a short program you wrote for use on its own can later turn out to be useful as a subprogram in another program. You might have written a SINC program, as above, just to calculate SINC functions, then later you will find that a program you are writing needs to use SINC - the SINC program becomes a subprogram used by the new program. The word "routine" is often used to describe something that can be a program <u>or</u> a subprogram.

It is worth making a collection of general-purpose routines which can be used by more than one program. An example is a routine which lets programs ask for some input. You might have a program which asks for a number in one place and asks a YES/NO question somewhere else. Instead of writing each question separately, you could write a routine which prompts the user to type in an answer. A program might ask for a number as below and add it to another number (note the ellipsis symbols .... are used to show there are other pieces of program before and after what is shown here):

    .... "What is X?" 1 DISP HALT + ...

Later some other program might ask if an answer is accurate enough:

```
... 4  DISP  "Is answer in level 1 OK?"
    1  DISP  HALT  "Y"  ==  ...
```

In both cases, the program has written out a question, displayed it in line 1 of the display (1 DISP), then stopped (HALT) to wait for an answer. You could put the three steps into a separate routine and use that routine whenever you need to ask a question:

```
<<  1  DISP  HALT  >>  P  R  M  T  STO
```

This creates a new command called PRMT which you can use whenever you want to prompt the user of a program to give an answer. The first program would now have:

```
....  "What is X?"  PRMT  +  ....
```

When the user sees the question, he or she must type in the answer, then press CONT to let the program continue. As stated above, a routine like this is in effect a new HP-28 command. (The HP-28 does not have a PRMT command built into it; the HP-28 idea is that you should put all your inputs on the stack before you start using a program - this is the way commands such as integration work, and this is the way the designers expect users to write programs most of the time. The PRMT command just described however lets you customize your HP-28 to work in a way more similar to that of the HP-41 which uses a PROMPT function to let a program ask for more information.) Once PRMT is written, you can use it in other programs; say you later need a program which asks how many yards of your road British Gas had dug up this morning. You could write a program which includes:

```
....  "BG yards?"  PRMT  "yd"  "m"  CONVERT
      SWAP  ->STR  SWAP  +  PR1 ....
```

You might not like the way PRMT behaves - Bruce Bailey has pointed out that users might be surprised when the question disappears as soon as they begin to give an answer, and might not like having to press the rather awkward and not at all obvious combination SHIFT 1 to continue the program. You could rewrite PRMT to suit your preferences, or you could wait until point 3.10 which shows a trick to customize CONT. If you have an HP-28S then Chapter 27 of the Owner's Manual shows other ways of asking for input.

An important use of subprograms is when a program needs to repeat something many times. If you use a program structure such as FOR...STEP or START...NEXT to repeat a set of commands then you can replace the whole set with one command which is itself a subprogram containing those commands. This makes it easier to test the set of commands, for example it is very important that the commands in a loop should not increase or decrease the number of objects on the stack. If you want to display the square roots of all the whole numbers from 1 to 1000 you must be very careful not to end up leaving a copy of each square root on the stack - an HP-28C would run out of room long before you had put 1000 numbers on the stack.

2.12 Set your modes. One way to customize your HP-28 is to set the User Flags to some special combination which sets your preferred modes. You can save the settings of all your flags by using RCLF (in the Program Test menu) to get a binary number with all your flag settings. Then you can change some of the modes, and later get all the modes back to your preferred set-up by using this binary number and STOF. You might even like to save the binary number in a variable and recall it whenever you need to put back your modes.

Let us see how we can simplify this by writing a program to do all this at the press of a single key. An easy way to do this is to save the flags in a variable, then write a program to restore them from that variable:

a. Set all your preferred modes; angles, display, error handling etc.
b. Use RCLF to get all the flag settings. This brings all the flag settings to level 1 of the stack as a 64-bit number.
c. Do 64 STWS (so all 64 flags will be maintained).
d. Type F L A G S STO to put the settings in a variable called FLAGS.
e. Now do: << FLAGS STOF >> S E T M STO to create the command

SETM which sets all the modes to your preferred combination at the press of one key.

RCLF, STOF, RCL and STO recall and store all 64 flags even if the binary word size is not 64, but accidentally editing a binary number can lose part of it, so the word size is set to 64 just in case, before the binary number is stored, but after your original word size has been recorded by RCLF.

Creating two variables, FLAGS and SETM, is something of a nuisance and a waste of space. It would be much neater to have the binary number right there in the program. You can do this easily!

a. Set all your modes.

b. Do RCLF to recall all 64 flags as a binary number.

c. Set the binary word size to 64 bits: 64 STWS.

d. Press EDIT; now you have the whole binary number in the command line.

e. Press INS and put << in front of the binary number.

f. Press SHIFT > (the RIGHT key) to go past its right hand end.

g. Press SPACE S T O F ENTER

h. This has created a program containing the binary number; you can store the program and the binary number in one variable: ' S E T M STO.

Now you can press USER and SETM to restore modes controlled by user flags and the word size; we have used EDIT to build a program around the binary number which holds the flag settings. This time we have to set the word size to 64 so the whole binary number will be displayed and edited.

2.13 Putting non-keyable characters in programs. You can use a trick similar to the above to put non-keyable characters into a program. Say you want to write a program to display a time as "HH:MM:SS". The colon can not be entered directly from the keyboard - there is no key for it. One way to do this would be to use the command CHR to put a colon into level 1:

.... STD DUP IP ->STR 58 CHR + ...

would take the integer part of a number, turn it into a text string, then create character number 58, which is a colon (see table in the description of STRING), then add the colon after the number. If you were going to do this a lot of times you might write a special program to put a colon in the stack:

<< 58 CHR >> C O L O N STO

You could use this command, COLON, to put a colon onto the stack whenever you need it, for example the program above would become:

.... STD DUP IP ->STR COLON + ...

but it is even better to put a colon right into your program. To write the same program as above and put a colon into it, do the following:

1. Write the program as far as the command before the colon:

<< .... STD DUP IP ->STR

2. Press ENTER to put the program so far into level 1 of the stack.

3. Do ->STR, this turns the program into a text string:

"<< .... STD DUP IP ->STR >>"

4. Do 58 CHR to put a colon into level 1.

5. Press + to add the colon to the end of the program, you now have:

"<< .... STD DUP IP ->STR >>:"

6. Press EDIT, delete the quote at the beginning of the program and replace the >> with a quote ", this leaves you with the command line containing the program:

<< .... STD DUP IP ->STR ":"

Now you can carry on writing the rest of the program. Instead of using a subprogram for the colon, or 58 CHR , you have ":" right in the program. Not only is this clearer; you see the character itself, it also saves seven bytes for every non-keyable character entered this way instead of by use of CHR.

Putting further non-keyable characters into the program is more difficult as it already has quotes ["] in it and these will split the program if you edit it again. One way out is to put place markers where you want special characters, and to put in all the characters at one time, at the very end, putting the final program together from several text strings, with special characters between them, and EDITing the final string into a program.

A similar technique was used by many HP-41 owners; it was much neater to have special non-keyable characters included in a text string in a program, rather than to create them with XTOA (an HP-41 extended function which did the same as CHR). Unfortunately, getting non-keyable characters into HP-41 programs was difficult: techniques called Synthetic Programming, special barcodes, or special plug-in modules had to be used. The HP-28 cannot read barcode or have modules plugged into it, but it does let you put special characters into a program, thus letting you customize your programs easily.

2.14 Subprograms and local variables. The notes on local names and local variables at the end of the section on Programs in the Reference Manual deserve to be read very carefully. Local variables (already mentioned in points 2.7 and 2.8) make it easier to write programs which use objects from the stack, as the examples in the Reference Manual make clear. Programs which use local variables instead of duplicating objects on the stack and moving the stack around are usually clearer and easier to understand, but they often take up more of the HP-28 memory. You can decide whether you find it easier to use local variables or to juggle objects on the stack - yet another case of customizing your use of the HP-28.

It is important to avoid confusing local variables and their names with ordinary, or "global" variables. A local variable is recognized only within the program where it was created. (If another program creates a local variable with the same name, then the second program will have a completely separate local variable, and when that program finishes, then its local variable will vanish.) Suppose you write and store a program T1:

<< -> A << A SQ A INV + >> >> 'T1 STO

T1 will calculate $X^2 + 1/X$ where X is the object in level 1 of the stack. Suppose though, that you already have a separate program called TT which does this job:

<< A SQ A INV + >> 'TT STO

You might want to make the program T1 shorter by using TT:

<< -> A << TT >> >> 'T1 STO

The program TT was written separately from T1, so it expects to use a global variable called A, not a local variable. If you do not have an ordinary variable called A then this second version of T1 will give the algebraic answer 'SQ(A)+INV(A)' , this is very neat and correct, but it might not be the answer you expect. Even worse, if an ordinary variable called A does exist, then that will be used when the answer is worked out, so you might not notice that anything has gone wrong (until your bridge falls down or your experimental airplane loses its wings). To help you avoid any such horrible possibilities, the Reference Manual suggests that you use lower case letters for local names, and upper case letters for global variables. In that case, T1 would be:

<< -> a << TT >> >>

and TT would still be:

<< A SQ A INV + >>

There would be far less chance of confusing the local variable 'a' with the global variable called 'A'.

What if you <u>wanted</u> TT to work with a local variable though? You might want to write a subprogram which <u>can</u> be used from within T1. You could write the program:

<< a SQ a INV + >> 'TT STO

but this would still expect to use a global variable called 'a'. You can force it to use a local variable instead by writing the program while a local variable 'a' exists. To do this you must

write TT, or edit it, while a program which uses the local variable
'a' is halted. Write the following:

1 -> a << HALT

then press ENTER. You will have created a program with the local
variable 'a', and the program will be HALTed, so that 'a' still
exists. (Observe that you do not need to put everything into a
program, the command line is treated as a program anyway when you
press ENTER.) The suspended program annunciator will be turned on
in the display, and 'a' will have the value 1; it does not really
matter what is in 'a', the purpose of the 1 is only to prevent 'a'
trying to take something off the stack. Now you can write:

<< a SQ a INV + >> 'TT STO

and in future this program will expect 'a' to be a local variable,
because the program was written while a local variable 'a' existed.
(Press CONT to finish the HALTed program.) If TT has already been
written, you can VISIT it, then press ENTER. VISITing the program
turns it into a text string, it "decompiles" the program. Pressing
ENTER turns the text string back into a program, it "compiles" the
program. (Note: If you press ATTN then the decompiled program is
ignored, and the original compiled version is kept.) Now that TT
has been made to expect a local variable, it will not be able to use
a global variable 'a', but it will be able to use a local variable
when a program creates this local variable and then carries out the
command TT. If you edit the subprogram later, when there is no
suspended program containing 'a', the subprogram will go back to
treating 'a' as an ordinary variable; so to look at the subprogram
TT, RCL a copy to the stack, do not VISIT it. ("Ordinary" names are
not really "global" on the HP-28S, as will be explained in Chapter
5.)

This whole subject was raised in a letter from Jean-Daniel Dodin to
the leader of the HP-28 design team, Dr. Bill Wickes. Bill Wickes
pointed out that a subprogram would be able to use local variables
if it was compiled in a HALTed environment containing the desired
local names. My thanks go to Bill Wickes, to Jean-Daniel Dodin for
showing me their correspondence on the subject, and to Bruce Bailey
for pointing out the possible confusion depending on whether a

program is compiled when a local variable does or does not exist. Bill Wickes' original point was that there are two ways to let separate subprograms share a local variable. One method is to let the first subprogram leave a copy of its local variable on the stack, and to make the second subprogram pick up the object from the stack, the other is to compile the subprograms in a HALTed environment containing that local variable. Say you have a program such as T1 above:

<< -> a << a SQ a INV + >> >>

You might want to split the subprogram into two subprograms TT1 and TT2:

<< a SQ >> 'TT1 STO   and   << a INV >> 'TT2 STO

The main program would become:

<< -> a << TT1 TT2 + >> >>

Clearly you would want both TT1 and TT2 to recognize the local variable 'a' and the method described above would allow this. In real life there would be little point in splitting up such a short program, but if you write a long subprogram you might well need to split it up into smaller parts so that you can edit it without running out of memory.

One more warning: in point 2.6 above I suggested that you can write alternative versions of HP-28 commands, and give each the same name as the built-in HP-28 command, but with part of the name in lower case letters. I have also repeated the HP suggestion of using lower case letters for local names and upper case letters for ordinary variables. To avoid confusion I suggest you stick to the following rules:

1. For local variable names use lower case letters only. Avoid 'i' and 'e' as these are the names of commands. 'I' and 'J' are exceptions to this rule; many programmers (including me) use I and J as loop counters, so use these as local loop counters and avoid using them as global names.
2. For ordinary (global) names use upper case letters only, except I and J.

3. For names of variables which replace HP-28 commands, begin with an upper case letter and put the rest of the name in lower case letters.

2.15 Complex numbers and arrays. In HP-28 arithmetic, real numbers are treated as complex numbers with the imaginary part missing. Thus:

$$1 \quad ENTER \quad (2,3) \quad +$$

gives the answer (3,3) as expected. Furthermore, 1 IM gives 0, which is indeed the imaginary part of (1,0), and -1 SQRT gives (0,1). In effect, the HP-28 is able to turn a real number into a complex number when this is necessary. The same usually works for vectors and matrices, try entering the matrix: [[1 2] [3 5]] , then EDIT it to change the first element from 1 to (1,2), and press ENTER. The whole matrix will automatically be turned into a complex matrix.

If you specifically want to turn a real array into a complex array (e.g. to let you PUT complex values into a real array), you can do the following:

1. Recall the array to level 1.
2. Press ENTER to make a second copy.
3. Press 0 CON to set all the elements of the copy to zero.
4. Press R->C to create the complex array, with imaginary parts of 0.

2.16 Algebra with binary numbers. The HP-28 will not let you use binary numbers in algebraic expressions, you cannot type in: '#1 AND #2'. Fortunately, you can write 'A AND B', and evaluate it even if either A or B or both contain binary numbers. Thus, if you want to do some masking calculations, picking out only the first and third bytes of a four-byte binary number in hexadecimal notation, you could store the mask:

$$\#FF00FF00 \quad M \quad A \quad S \quad K \quad STO$$

Then you could type in your binary number, store it, and do the masking:

$$\#56789ABC \quad 'B \quad STO \quad 'B \quad AND \quad MASK' \quad EVAL$$

Mind you, only users of TI or Casio calculators are likely to need this, users of the HP-16C know how to do binary arithmetic in stack notation.

2.17 Storing data in numbered registers and on the stack. Unlike earlier HP calculators the HP-28 uses named variables instead of numbered registers. This is often easier, but it can cause trouble if you want to translate an HP-41 program to run on the HP-28. The makers recognized this problem and suggested a way round it; Appendix B in the HP-28C Reference Manual and in the HP-28S Owner's Manual provide programs NRCL and NSTO which recall and store values in numbered registers, for example   17.5   3   NSTO   will store the value 17.5 in register 3, just like   17.5   STO 3 on the HP-41.

NRCL and NSTO have two shortcomings. One is that they make no provision for a register 0. To deal with this put   1   +   at the beginning of both programs. The other worry is that NRCL and NSTO use a matrix called 'REG', so they can only store real numbers. You may prefer to rewrite the programs to use a list called 'REG' instead of a matrix, then other objects such as complex numbers can be stored and recalled.

The HP-41 allows the user to store numbers and text strings into any of the stack registers X, Y, Z, T, L and also into the synthetically accessible stack registers M, N, and so on. Values stored in these registers can also be recalled from them. The HP-28 lets you recall objects from any stack level by means of PICK, but there is no simple way to store an object in a selected stack level. You can use VISIT to edit the contents of any stack level (for example   9   VISIT   lets you edit the 9th stack level), but this is not the same as storing the object in level 1 in some other stack level.

If the name for a command which picks the nth object in the stack is PICK, then PLACE would be a suitable name for a command which places an object in the nth position. Here is a PLACE program, printed on several lines, with explanations at the right of each line. The program is designed to place a new object in level n of the stack. The stack diagram for PLACE is:

PLACE

Level n+2 ...	Level 3	Level 2	Level 1		Level n ...	Level 1
obj n	obj 1	new obj	n	->	new obj	obj 1

```
<< -> n                    ;Save n in a local variable
 << n ->LIST               ;Put n objects in a list,
                           ;error if n too small
   IF  DEPTH 1 > n         ;If more than 1 object on stack
     AND                   ;and n not zero:
     THEN  SWAP  DROP      ;Then OK, so remove object n,
       n  GETI             ;pick new object from the list,
       SWAP  DROP  SWAP    ;drop the GETI counter,
                           ;put new obj above list,
     LIST-> DROP2          ;turn list back to stack,
                           ;drop n & new obj copy.
     ELSE  "Nonexistent"   ;Else say stack level n is nonexistent,
       1  DISP             ;display the message in line 1
                           ;of display,
       LIST->              ;and put back the stack objects,
                           ;new obj and n.
   END                     ;End the IF THEN ELSE construct.
>>  >>                     ;Finish local variable structure
                           ;and program.
```

This program is rather long because it deals with errors such as n being the wrong type or zero or larger than the number of objects in the stack. Trying to write a shorter version would be a good programming exercise.

Most HP calculators also have a command to exchange the contents of register X (equivalent to level 1) with the contents of any numbered register. You could replace this on the HP-28 with:

```
<< DUP NRCL ROT ROT NSTO >> 'NSWP STO
```

If you manipulate the stack a lot then remember to check for commands that make this easier. For example OVER which copies the object from level 2 is often overlooked by users. (Sorry about the pun!)

2.18 Tidying up memory, and the USER menu. By the time you have written a few programs and stored a few variables in an HP-28C the USER menu can look quite a mess and you may well be short of memory. Use the last line of the USER menu and the keyboard operations provided to help you tidy up USER and memory; in addition there is an automatic Out of Memory procedure. (See Appendix B for a warning about the Out of Memory procedure.)

If you have a lot of programs on an HP-28C, you might like to group them into related sets - you can do this with ORDER. On an HP-28S you can use subdirectories instead, but ORDER has other uses, for example in programs. Say you have a new program called NEW which you use all the time and which you want to be on the leftmost menu key. If the program does some statistics or plotting it might create a new statistics matrix or a list of plot parameters and put them on the leftmost key. To make sure your program stays on the leftmost key despite this, you can finish it with the commands:

.... { NEW } ORDER >>

If you think you might be running out of memory you can use MEM to see how many free bytes you have left. The automatic memory warnings begin to show up all the time if you have less than 128 bytes free; if you are approaching this limit then you should delete your stack variables, either all of them with CLEAR, or at least some of them. Better still, PURGE some of your variables, or be really brave and delete them all with CLUSR! This is such a dramatic step that the HP-28 gives you a chance to change your mind when you press CLUSR from the USER menu. Remember you can give PURGE a list of variables to purge, instead of purging them one by one.

2.19 Playing with Menus. ORDER and PURGE give you considerable control over the USER menu on an HP-28C; you have more control on the HP-28S, as will be described in Chapter 5. Other menus are less under your control: you can move through them with NEXT and PREV, in FORM within ALGEBRA the menus available depend on the expression you are positioned at. In the MODE menu, your current modes are highlighted on an HP-28C, or marked with a square on an HP-28S, and in the SOLVR menu, the names of your variables are shown. One very useful extra is the ability to let programs select which menu to display. If for instance you HALT a program, it would be useful to let that program select the PROGRAM CONTROL menu for you, so that you could immediately use SST to single step through the program. The HP-28S command MENU lets you do this, we shall see in point 3.11 how this sort of thing can be done on an HP-28C.

2.20 One-command programs. A final tip for this chapter. Point 2.6 described a simple way to put the command IP (and others) on the USER menu. The method described there puts a whole program in the variable 'Ip', this stores the command IP but takes extra nybbles to mark the beginning and end of the program. It is possible to store the command itself in a variable using a trick discovered by Graeme Cawsey.

1. Type { IP and press ENTER. This creates the list { IP }.
2. Type 1   GET and press ENTER. This extracts the first object from   the list, in this case that object is the command IP all on its own. 3. Type 'Ip   STO.   This stores the command IP in the variable Ip with fewer "overheads" than a complete program, saving 14 nybbles.

You can use the new variable 'Ip' just as described in point 2.6, and you can use Graeme's trick to save 14 nybbles when storing any single command. A good use for this is to store the command SYSEVAL in a variable called S (compare this with point 1.6) and it will be useful in the next chapter.

CHAPTER 3 - USING SYSEVAL

Little is said in the manuals about the SYSEVAL command, but that little suggests SYSEVAL can do a great deal for anyone wanting to customize their HP-28. This chapter shows some uses of SYSEVAL. At the same time, you will see how SYSEVAL can let you learn about the internal workings of the HP-28. Information discovered this way can lead to more uses of SYSEVAL, and to tricks needed to let you write machine code programs.

3.1 Version numbers. The only use of SYSEVAL described in the manuals is to find which version of the HP-28 you have. The manuals tell you to execute #10 SYSEVAL to display the version number of your HP-28 on the top line of the display. To restore the normal display, just press ATTN. SYSEVAL is not in any menu, you must spell it out or fetch it from the COMMAND list. If you use HEX mode for binary operations, remember to execute #A SYSEVAL instead. Actually, calling objects such as #10 or #A by the name "binary integer" can be confusing, since they are binary integers when displayed in BIN mode, but should really be called hexadecimal integers when displayed in HEX mode. On the HP-28S a "b", "o", "d" or "h" is put after all binary integers to show their base, and you can enter a binary integer in any base by putting the appropriate letter after it. In general, I shall use HEX mode in the rest of this book, so "binary integer" will mean an HP-28 binary value displayed in HEX; I shall usually write binary integers with an "h". HP-28S owners can enter all binary integers as given here and follow them with an "h". HP-28C users should ignore the "h" but remember to set HEX mode - those who dislike hexadecimal can set HEX mode before entering any binary integer given here and return to their preferred mode afterwards - you could even write a program to do this.

Finding the version number of a calculator or computer can be important, since subtle changes are made from one version to the next, and you might take a long time to notice that a program written on one version behaves differently on another. The internal details of the operating system of a calculator are usually a company secret and HP does not always publicize the details of changes from one version to another. One good reason for belonging to a user club is that members will swap information on such changes, and sometimes HP gives the clubs details of changes. At other times HP does not even tell the users that a change has been made. In the case of the HP-41, it was very difficult to find what version you had (you had to use Synthetic Programming or a special diagnostic plug-in module to check it). With the HP-71, there is an official instruction, VER$, which anyone can use to check the version of their HP-71. With the HP-28, HP has taken a half-way position, there is no command like VER$, but they do provide a way to find the version number with SYSEVAL.

The first version of the HP-28 that was sold was version 1BB of the HP-28C. (If you have an earlier version then you should have been writing this chapter!) Version 1BB was sold for about the first three quarters of 1987. This was followed by version 1CC in late 1987, then version 2BB of the HP-28S in early 1988; further versions may come out later. Most of this book applies to all types and versions of the HP-28, but the SYSEVAL addresses given in this chapter and the next are specific to version 1BB. Check your version and if it is not 1BB then find the corresponding addresses in Appendix E. The one address that cannot change from version to version is #Ah (remember I am using HEX), since that has to be the same in all versions so you can use it to find what version you have.

Note that you can use #Ah SYSEVAL in a running program. The program will carry on running but will not change the display after the version has been put in the top line. To restore the display to normal, put CLMF (clear message flag) into your program, or press ATTN when the program stops.

3.2 The system clock. HP have released few other addresses for use with SYSEVAL. One is the address which gives you a number that represents the system clock; the number is incremented 8192 times a second. The HP-28 manuals do not describe this clock, but they do admit one exists - the description of RDZ (Randomize) says the system clock can be used as a seed for the random number generator. In addition, the clock is used to turn the HP-28 off if it has not been used for 10 minutes, and for timing the rate at which information is sent to the printer. Unfortunately the designers put in so many other functions that they did not get round to providing commands to set and use the clock.

To read the system clock, just execute #123Eh SYSEVAL (see Appendix E if you do not have version 1BB) or write a program << # 123Eh SYSEVAL >> and use that. The result does not look particularly useful, it is a binary integer. If you repeat exactly the same operation though, the second result will be different from the first; it is a second clock reading - it should be larger than the first - if it is not then you probably have a small wordsize set - to avoid losing information from the clock it is best to set the wordsize to 64 bits by doing 64 STWS . Every time you repeat #123Eh SYSEVAL you should get another larger number, the difference between each pair of numbers is the number of times that the clock value has increased by 1 count, at the rate of 8192 counts per second.

Try the following: store the program << # 123Eh SYSEVAL >> in a variable called T, then press the key marked T twice in rapid succession. (If you do not have version 1BB replace #123E with the address in Appendix E.) Now SWAP the two numbers, subtract the first from the second, and use B->R to turn the result to a decimal number. Unless you do something unusual, the result is unlikely ever to be much below 1500. Now 1500/8192 represents just under 0.2 seconds, so this is the fastest rate at which you can expect to repeatedly press a key on your HP-28. This is not quite as fast as on other calculators, and is due to the keys on the HP-28 being much stiffer than on most calculators. If you try this several times you will sometimes see a much larger interval - this will happen if the HP-28 has to do something else between dealing with the two keystrokes. For example the clock might have updated itself by a full minute, or some tidying up of the memory might have been done, or the HP-28 might have just been woken from being dormant after being unused for a while. The exact timing depends on the stiffness of the keys on your HP-28, the time increases with the number of objects already on the stack, and if COMMAND, UNDO and LAST are enabled.

You can use this to time other things too - to check how long different commands take, or to time a complete program. Say you have two versions of a program - P1 and P2 - you can compare them with the program:

<pre>
        << #123Eh SYSEVAL 'TMP' STO P1
        #123Eh SYSEVAL TMP - B->R 8192 / >>
</pre>

This will tell you how long the program took in seconds. Repeat the same for P2 and you will know which is faster. It is best to try timing each program more than once, as the HP-28 sometimes interrupts programs to tidy up its memory, which can make a program seem to run longer (this tidying up of memory is called "garbage collection"). When timing a program which does some printing wait a while for any previous printing to finish - otherwise the timing may be slowed down because the HP-28 slows down to wait for the printer to catch up. (The HP-28S is faster than the HP-28C.)

An obvious thing to try is to use the system clock to tell you the time. The system clock usually starts up at some random value when the first batteries are put in, so the time it gives will not be correct. That means you will have to add a correction to the system clock to get the real time. The system clock is stored to sufficient accuracy that you can time things to well below a second and yet still run it for several hundred years, so you can use it to get dates as well, and if you just want a time then you need to round it to the nearest second and get the hour modulo 24. The program shown below does all that, of course you can equally well use the clock to keep track of the date, or to provide a stopwatch.

Steps	Comments and explanations
<< #123Eh SYSEVAL B->R	;Begin program, read clock, turn to ;real no.
29491199 / KOR +	;convert to hour and fraction, add ;correction
->HMS 24 MOD	;turn to 24 hour clock value HHMMSS
DUP IP ->STR ":" +	;get "HH:" part
SWAP FP ->STR	;turn fractional part into a string
DUP 2 3 SUB ":" +	;get "MM:" part
SWAP 4 5 SUB + + >>	;get "SS", create "HH:MM:SS", finish.
'TIME' STO	;store the program called TIME
0 'KOR' STO	;store a correction of 0

This program assumes you have set the binary word size to 64 and the display mode to STD or FIX n where n is greater than 3; you can include these requirements in the program, or write another program to deal with this, see below. Point 2.13 in the previous chapter showed how you can put a colon into a program. To get the value of KOR, type in a time HH.MMSS about 30 seconds ahead of the present, wait for that time to arrive, then press TIME. Now EDIT the time in level 1 to turn it into another number HH.MMSS (remove the quotes around it, turn the first : into a radix mark, and remove the second :) then do HMS- to get the correction. Add 24 to it if this is negative, then use HMS-> to convert it to hours and a fraction of an hour, and store this in KOR. Now use TIME again and make any small corrections to KOR if you wish.   The system clock is controlled by a quartz oscillator and should be accurate to within a few seconds a month.

If you just want to see the time, press TIME, but if you want a running clock you can write another program which uses TIME, and which also sets the correct binary wordsize and display mode:

Steps	Comments and explanations
<< RCLF	;Begin program, get current flag ;status
64 STWS STD	;set binary word size and display mode
DO	;begin a loop to display the time
TIM 1 DISP	;get the time and display it on line 1
UNTIL	;test if the loop is to be repeated
KEY	;the test is to see if a key has been ;pressed
END	;if so then finish the loop
DROP STOF >>	;drop the key name, replace flags, ;finish
'CLOCK' STO	;store the program

Now you can press CLOCK and see a running clock in the first line of the display. The clock might not advance quite smoothly, as the loop takes about one third of a second to repeat, so at times the clock display will advance by a second after three steps through the loop, and at other times it will advance after only two steps. You could try to rewrite the programs to make them shorter and faster so the clock will run more smoothly. To stop the clock, press any key except ATTN, and press ATTN to clear the clock value from the top line of the display.

As with the version number, you can use SYSEVAL with #123E to get the clock from a running program. This is very important - binary numbers which work with SYSEVAL but stop a running program are less useful.

If you do a memory reset (Memory Lost) on your HP-28, you will find that the clock has not been reset to zero - it carries on running, although the correction might have to be changed by a value no larger than a minute. This shows Memory Lost is not really a memory lost - various pointers are reset inside the HP-28 to show there is no usable information in the stack and variables, but many numbers, including the clock, are not changed.

3.3 A programmable SHIFT. The first two points have shown interesting uses of SYSEVAL which HP has released. Now let us begin looking at uses which HP has not told us of. To begin with, here is a simple example:

<< #9C96h SYSEVAL >> 'SHIFT' STO

This creates a program which does the same as the shift key! (Remember to look up the equivalent to #9C96 in Appendix E if you do not have version 1BB.) The shift key is not programmable, but you can include this SHIFT subprogram in other programs. That might be fun, but is it useful?

One possible use would be if you know that after a program finishes you will want to select a new menu. Say you select the USER menu and run a program which finishes by leaving a new object on the stack, and you know you will need to select the ALGEBRA menu next to examine this object, or the PRINT menu to print it. Putting SHIFT at the end of the program will save you having to press shift before pressing a key to select a menu. This might be useful to some people, to others it will be of interest only as a curiosity or to impress their friends. Let us look at another use:

<< #9C96h SYSEVAL 1 WAIT #9CA3h SYSEVAL >>

is a program which sets shift, waits for a second, then clears shift again. This shows you can use #9C96h at any place in a program to set the shift annunciator, and #9CA3h at any time to clear the shift annunciator. Now, the HP-41 had five special annunciators 0, 1, 2, 3, 4 which could be set at any place in a program to show some special condition was in effect. For example, you could set flag 00 and thus turn on the annunciator marked 0 to tell the user that a crucial part of a program was in progress and that the program should not be interrupted. The HP-28 does not have such special annunciators, but knowing the addresses just given you can use SYSEVAL to turn the shift annunciator on and off, using it like an HP-41 flag display.

WARNING: Interrupting programs which use SYSEVAL can be dangerous.

If you interrupt such a program or if it goes wrong before finishing then be sure the binary word size and flags are put back to their original settings - do not ask HP for help with SYSEVAL values they have not released.

3.4 A bit more memory? If you run out of memory the first thing to do is to delete unwanted variables. Then you clear the stack, then disable LAST, UNDO and COMMAND. If you still have too little space for a long program on an HP-28C, try doing:

1 #11AA SYSEVAL

This releases 50 extra bytes, by freeing some of the memory used for things such as error messages and statistics information. The 1 is needed because #11AA SYSEVAL drops the stack by one level. The extra 50 bytes will in many cases be just enough to let you enter an unusually long program.   To restore the original status of the calculator, do a System Halt (ON UP).

You might be worried that such cavalier use of SYSEVAL could do some damage to the HP-28.   Fortunately SYSEVAL can alter only the contents of RAM, and thus the display and the beeper, but it cannot damage the hardware of the HP-28. The worst that can happen is that the HP-28 will hang up - stop working normally, and that can usually be remedied with a System Halt. If a System Halt does not work, then try a Memory Reset (ON INS RIGHT), and if that fails too then take the batteries out, replace them, and try again.

3.5 Playing with SYSEVAL. How can you find useful SYSEVAL numbers such as those given just above?   One method is simply trial and error, and indeed many early discoveries were made that way.   What can we learn just by using SYSEVAL without help from HP? To begin with, the HP-18 and HP-28 were developed after the HP-71B, and it was believed they used the same basic chip, or CPU. The internal design specifications (IDS) of the HP-71B are available (at a total price greater than that of the 71 itself!), so it is possible to check if the HP-28 is similar to the HP-71B. One of the things you can find from the HP-71B IDS is that the HP-71B CPU (called the Saturn) uses 20-bit addresses.   This means that addresses are binary numbers 20 bits long. If the HP-28 uses the same CPU and addressing then addresses used by the HP-28 will also be 20-bit binary integers, and any bits past the 20th will simply be ignored. We can check this by taking the address #Ah and writing it in binary: #1010b, then turning it into a 21-bit number with the leftmost bit set as well:

#100000000000000001010b (use BIN mode on an HP-28C)

Put this into level 1, then execute SYSEVAL. Indeed you will see the version number displayed again. This leads to several points:

1. Clearly the HP-28 uses 20-bit addresses, just like the HP-71B. If you try a 20-bit long number with the leftmost bit set then you will not see the version number displayed, but if you try a 22-bit number with the leftmost bit set then once again you will see the version number.

2. The above confirms that the HP-28 uses a CPU similar to that of the HP-71B. Indeed, HP has now stated that the CPU of the HP-18B, the HP-19B, the HP-28C and the HP-28S is a modified Saturn CPU.

3. It is also reasonable to believe that the binary number used by SYSEVAL is quite simply a 20-bit address at which SYSEVAL expects to find a subprogram to be executed. The design team leader, Bill Wickes, has given some more details of this in talks to a group of user club members.

If the HP-28 has similarities to the HP-71B then the operating system (the program which controls the HP-28) begins at address #0. As HP has said that the operating system is 128K bytes long, it must finish at address #3FFFF and between these two there are 262,144 possible addresses which can be checked with SYSEVAL (each address points to a nybble, which is half a byte, so there are twice as many addresses as there are bytes). Beyond address #3FFFF there must be addresses where the display information is held and where the stack and user variables are stored. This kind of information changes, so it must be kept in a type of memory which can be changed - this is called Random Access Memory (RAM) - it is memory which you can read and write, selecting addresses at random as you need them. The HP-28 operating system does not change and is stored in memory called ROM - Read Only Memory. Any search must examine not only all 262,144 ROM addresses, it must also find and examine the RAM addresses.

A hit and miss search of the whole of ROM is too much for one person, but a limited search of selected areas by a group can find enough information that a full search is no longer needed. Many HP-28 owners began at #0 and went upwards, looking for anything interesting. Some shared their results through user groups, and understood better what was happening. On the other hand, it seems equally possible that the top of ROM will also have interesting addresses; two people in the UK started from that end - and Ian Maw soon made a very useful discovery which will be described next.

First though, if you are going to use SYSEVAL frequently then to save spelling it out each time do << SYSEVAL >> 'S' STO, and press S instead of SYSEVAL.

3.6 A generalized STO. The STO command needs a name object in level 1 and any object in level 2. The name in level 1 is used to create a variable name, and the object in level 2 is stored in that variable. What Ian Maw found was that #3FBA7 SYSEVAL works just like STO, but does not check that the object in level 1 really is a name. This discovery led to two new possibilities. One is that variables can be created with names which could not be made by normal means. The second is that objects in the stack can be turned into variable names, and then those names can be brought to the command line and studied - thus objects can be turned into name strings and their structure can be analyzed. This second is not directly relevant to this book; it has been described in articles in user club magazines, some details of object structures found this way are described in Appendix C.

Creating a name which cannot be made by normal means can be a useful form of customization. Imagine you use the constant 12345 a great deal - you can store it in a variable called CONST, but wouldn't it be nice to store it in a variable called '12345'? The STO command will not let you create a variable with a name like this, but the generalized STO will let you do so.

A name object consists of a 5-nybble long address, followed by two nybbles which give the length NN of the name, followed by NN bytes each of which is one character of the name. Each character is represented by its ASCII code, and the ASCII codes are stored internally as one byte each. A table of ASCII codes is given in the STRING section of the Reference Manual. (The codes are in decimal, you can convert them to hexadecimal with R->B.) The name 'ABCDE' would be:

```
2 1 D 2 0 5 0  1 4 2 4 3 4 4 4 5 4
\       /  \/  \/  \/  \/  \/  \/
 adr       len  A   B   C   D   E
```

Observe that the nybbles in each byte are swapped so you get the representation shown above.

A real number consists of a 5-nybble address followed by the number's 3-digit exponent and 12-digit mantissa, stored back to front. Thus the number

$$-7.46454443424E105$$

is stored as:

```
3 3 9 2 0  5 0 1  4 2 4 3 4 4 4 5 4 6 4 7   9
\     /  \ / \  /                     /  \/
 adr      exp        mantissa        sign:
                                     9 if negative
```

There is a SYSEVAL address which can let you check this. To see how, set STD mode, then type 1.23E87, then press ->STR. You will see "1.23E87". This is the string that represents the number. Now type in the same number again and do #2DF0B SYSEVAL. Once again you will see "1.23E87". #2DF0B is actually the address of a generalized ->STR command which converts the object in level 1 into a string representation of a number, without checking if the object really is a number. (This is a bit like the generalized STO described above which does not check if the object in level 1 is a name.) Now type ' A B C D E and ENTER - you have the name 'ABCDE' in level 1 of the stack. Do #2DF0B SYSEVAL. and 'ABCDE' is replaced by "-7.46454443424E105".

You can see that the name 'ABCDE' has been turned into the number described below it. Both the generalized STO and the generalized ->STR assume that the object in level 1 has already been checked. The checking is done by subprograms which look at the address in front of the name or number to check its type and the "generalized" STO and ->STR are subprograms which normally follow this check and simply do the STO or ->STR operation.

N.B. Remember that if you do not have a version 1BB HP-28C then you should not use the addresses given here but the corresponding ones in Appendix E.

If you look again at the way the name and number are stored, you will see that they are very similar. In fact you can work out a number which is similar to a name, and reverse the process just shown above, to create a name. Thus the name '12345' would be:

<pre>
     2 1 D 2 0 5 0 1 3 2 3 3 3 4 3 5 3
      \   / \/ \/ \/ \/ \/ \/
          adr   len 1   2   3   4   5
</pre>

Remember again that the nybbles in each byte are swapped so you get the representation shown above. Now you could set up a number which looks the same, for example:

$$1.00353433323E105$$

is stored as:

$$3392050132333435300010$$

If you put 12345 into level 2 of the stack, 1.00353433323E105 into level 1, and do #3FBA7 SYSEVAL then you will create a variable whose name is '12345' and which contains the number 12345. Try it!

You can use the same method to create other customized names for variables. If you are going to use the method often then create a special program   << #3FBA7 SYSEVAL >> and store it with the name 'Sto'. Write down the name you want as an ASCII string, then write down a number whose end part represents the same ASCII string, and use #3FBA7 SYSEVAL to create the variable. (Not all names can be represented by a number, since numbers can only contain the hexadecimal digits 0 to 9. If you want to create other names, wait until the point on Non-Normalized numbers.) Remember to put the object in level 2 and the number in level 1 before using Sto. Since Sto does not check for errors, it will try to create a new variable if the stack contains only one object, or even none at all. If you do this, the stack will probably end up full of things called "System Object". In that case, do a system halt (press ON and UP at the same time) to clear the stack and the display, then press USER to see the USER menu. Most names created with Sto cannot easily be PURGEd, because they are not recognized as names. After all, that is the point of Sto - to create non-standard names. CLUSR will delete these names (and all others!) or you can wait until you get an Out Of Memory and can delete variables by name through the automatic deletion offered by Out Of Memory. DATAFILE has published a special program written by Jean-Daniel Dodin to cause Out Of Memory and force the HP-28 to go through the names asking you which ones to delete.

Bruce Bailey has suggested that this Sto operation be called "Ianization" after its discoverer. Let us finish this section with one more example of Ianization. Suppose you want a variable called #A - its ASCII form would be 2341 and it is 2 bytes long, so it can be represented by a number such as:

$$1.00000000412E302$$

Remember that the nybbles of each byte must be swapped round! Put into level 2 the object you want to store, put into level 1 the number above, then press the Sto key.

3.7 Programming with UNDO and COMMAND. LAST can be used in programs to recover the arguments of the previous command and use them again, but UNDO and COMMAND cannot be used in programs. The

HP-28 designers considered this unnecessary, since UNDO recovers the stack as it was before the program began, and COMMAND recovers the command line, which is not affected by a running program. Still, UNDO can be useful in a program - for example if a program were to find a mistake it could use UNDO to recover the stack as it was at the beginning of the program, and try something different, or tell the user there was something wrong. Consider the program:

<< FACT SWAP EXP / >>

This might detect overflow or underflow errors in several places. You might like to use the IFERR...THEN...END program structure to check if an error has occurred, and if so to recover the stack and display a message.

<< IFERR FACT SWAP EXP / THEN
Undo "Check arguments" 1 DISP END >>

The Undo subprogram uses SYSEVAL of course:

<< # 329BE SYSEVAL >> 'Undo' STO

For the program shown above to work, flags 57, 58 and 59 - the Underflow, Overflow and Infinite Result flags should all be set. UNDO must be enabled as well of course, see below. UNDO recovers the stack as it was before the latest command, so if any arguments were still on the command line when the program was started then those arguments will be lost. Of course any arguments that were in the command line can be recovered with COMMAND. The following program does the same as COMMAND, but leaves its result in level 1, since the command line cannot be used during a running program anyway:

<< # 9476 SYSEVAL # 32311 SYSEVAL >> 'Comm' STO

Store this program, then type 1.23 and press ENTER. Now press Comm and you will see the text string "1.23" in level 1. This is just the text string that was most recently in the command line. If you press Comm a second time, you will see the program itself returned to the command line, since that was the next most recent thing in the command line. The "1.23" will not vanish as it would if you executed COMMAND itself, because it had been returned to level 1, not the command line. You can repeat Comm up to four times to bring back the four strings that were most recently in the command line, and leave them in the stack. You can use Comm from the keyboard as an alternative to COMMAND itself - to bring things onto the stack instead of the command line, or you can use it from a running program. One reason for using this has been mentioned in the description of Undo above. If you want to use a text string brought back to level 1 by Comm then you will probably need to use STR->, for instance the "1.23" used in the example at the beginning of this paragraph can be turned into a number with STR->.

Clearly these programmable versions of COMMAND and UNDO cannot work unless COMMAND and UNDO have been enabled. LAST can be enabled and disabled from a program by the setting and clearing of flag 31, but COMMAND and UNDO are enabled and disabled only by non-programmable operations in the MODE menu. The following four programs make these operations programmable:

         << # 7786 SYSEVAL >> 'Cmon' STO - COMMAND ON
         << # 77A8 SYSEVAL >> 'Cmof' STO - COMMAND OFF
         << # F412 SYSEVAL >> 'Unon' STO - UNDO ON
         << # F44E SYSEVAL >> 'Unof' STO - UNDO OFF

If you need to use any of these only rarely then you need not store them as programs, just include the binary number and SYSEVAL in your program.

3.8 'BIP' and error messages. When the HP-28 detects an error it makes a short sound and stores the error message and number. You could customize a program such as the one at the beginning of the previous point if it could provide its own short BEEP and error information when displaying the message "Check Arguments". Naturally you could write your own program to do this, but:

         << "A" # 30B7 SYSEVAL >> 'BIP' STO

sets up such a command for you. It uses the internal error BEEP and even sets the error number to be 7; this is not used by any HP-28 errors so you can use BIP to record the information that the most recent error was a custom-made error of your own. BIP does not record any error message, so there is no chance of your being confused by a wrong message.

Even if you do not plan to write your own customized error messages BIP can be useful as a short BEEP. If you want to confuse or annoy your friends, try replacing the text string "A" with an empty text string "" - don't worry though, the "Memory Lost" message is only a message, nothing else happens! "Memory Lost" is error message number 5, you can display the first four messages built into the HP-28 with the following:

#3327 SYSEVAL   Error number #1   "Insufficient Memory"
#3333 SYSEVAL   Error number #2   "Range Exception"
#333F SYSEVAL   Error number #3   "Undefined Local Name"
#334B SYSEVAL   Error number #4   "Undefined ROM Pointer"

There are no messages 6 or 7; BIP creates an artificial error 7 that can be used for customization as shown above. You may notice that messages 2 and 4 do not appear in the list given in Appendix A of the Reference Manual. Message 2 can be used for internal work by the operating system and it is available for a future model to handle arithmetic errors in a different way, message 4 refers to pointers used internally by the HP-28 but not available to users through the normal user interface. These two messages are one sign of the complexity built into the HP-28 operating system, but hidden from users because it is not accessible through the user interface, that part of the operating system which communicates with you, the user.

Other messages like this can be found too. If you want to create more of your own error numbers, or if you want to study the error messages built into the HP-28, then replace "A" in BIP with a real number. The exponent (power of 10) of that number will be used as an error number. Put 1E4 in place of "A" and then use BIP - you will see "Undefined ROM Pointer" and the error number returned by ERRN will be #4. Now try 1E6 and you will hear a "bip", but there will be no error message; there is no error 6 on the HP-28C (there is on the HP-28S). If you try a number without an exponent, say 1 or 2, then you will get no sound or message, because error 0 is treated as no error. If you want to carry on experimenting, try BIP with 1E125, and 1E126. The first gives error #125, "Command Stack Disabled", and the second gives error #126, "Edit line > 4096". This second error is another one that is missing from the HP-28C manual, and for a very interesting reason. The HP-28C operating system treats the command line as a special text string and can deal with a command line up to 4K (4096 bytes) long; a command line longer than this cannot be handled. In the HP-28C though there is only about 1.7K available to the user, so a command line 4K long cannot be made, and there is no need for this message. If you add extra memory to an HP-28C (see Chapter 5), you might encounter this message, though usually an HP-28C with extra memory just gets stuck if you try to edit a command line this long.

The HP-28 allows for exponents from -499 to 499. Negative exponents are stored as 1000 plus the negative exponent, so that the exponent of 1E-499 is stored as 501. Try BIP with the number 1E-499 instead of the "A", and you will get error number 501. This lets you look at error numbers from #501 to #999 but the exponent of a real number cannot contain the hexadecimal digits A to F, so you cannot get at messages such as #A01. The next point will show you how to create Non-Normalized numbers which can have such exponents.

3.9 Non-Normalized numbers and more about SYSEVAL. You may have noticed that the names used for COMMAND ON and other subprograms in point 3.7 are rather awkward. This is because names such as +CMD cannot be created by normal means - the sections on names in the HP-28C Reference Manual and in the HP-28S Owner's Manual explain that some characters cannot be used in names. This is because those characters are used for other purposes, for example an expression beginning with ' and containing + or - is automatically considered to be an algebraic expression, not a name. In point 3.6 above we have seen that normally impossible names can be created by means of "Ianization", however the characters that can be used in such names are still limited to ones which are made up of the hexadecimal digits 0 - 9. This means that the generalized STO on its own cannot be used to make a name such as +CMD, because the ASCII code for + is hexadecimal 2B.

The generalized STO uses a number to create a name, and numbers in the HP-28 are stored internally in a form called BCD (Binary Coded Decimal), already mentioned in points 3.6 and 3.7. As another example, the number pi*10^257 has the value
3.14159265359E257   and is stored as:

```
0  3 1 4 1 5 9 2 6 5 3 5 9    2 5 7
\/   \                       /   \ /
sign       mantissa          exponent
```

In fact the number is stored back to front, and with 33920 in front of it as was shown in point 3.6, but we can ignore that here. The 0 at the front denotes a positive number, a 9 would denote a negative number. As was explained in the previous point, the next twelve digits are the number's mantissa, and the last three digits are its exponent. If the power of 10 is a negative number then it is added to 1000 and the result is stored in the three digit exponent. This very neat scheme allows calculators to store decimal numbers with three-digit exponents between -499 and +500. The scheme does not expect any digits greater than 9, but hexadecimal digits A - F are available and could be put in a number unless it is converted to the standard form, i.e. "normalized". Similarly, the first digit of the mantissa is expected to be non-zero (unless the whole number is zero), since having the most significant digit of a number stored in the leftmost position makes calculations more efficient. Any number which has digits A - F in it or has zeros to the left of the most significant digit or has a sign that is not 0 or 9 is called a Non-Normalized number. HP calculators and pocket computers sometimes use such numbers, for instance to store hexadecimal numbers, to denote an infinite result, or a number which is smaller than 1.0E-499, but is not quite zero. Other HP calculators and computers are not designed to use Non-Normalized numbers (NNNs) but can create them and use them under certain conditions. One condition under which the HP-28 could use NNNs would be to create error message numbers such as #A01, see point 3.8 above. Another use would be to create additional non-standard names as just mentioned.

A fairly simple way to create a NNN is to build it up within a text string in a variable, then to bring it to the stack with SYSEVAL. The HP-28 memory layout (see also Appendix C) is such that variables are stored as shown here:

CONTENTS   **ADDRESS**

Contents	<---	Top nybble of user RAM, address #4FFFF
of the most		Next nybble down, #4FFFE
recently		Nybble #4FFFD
created		Lower nybbles
variable		.
		.
length of		.
variable's		.
name		(Note that the top of RAM is at a
		different address in the HP-28S - as
letters in		usual see Appendix E for details.)
the name		
Next		
variable		

If you put a text string in level 2 of the stack, a previously unused name in level 1, and press STO, then the text string will lie at the very top of the memory, and you will be able to work out where it is. To see this, put the string "XYZ" in level 2, put the name 'QQQ' in level 1, and do STO. The text string is 6 nybbles long (3 characters which is 3 bytes or 6 nybbles). Below this come 5 nybbles which give the length of the string, and then the 5 nybble address which defines the object to be a text string. That makes a total length of 16 nybbles, so the text string begins 15 nybbles below the top of memory, at address #4FFF0. Try doing #4FFF0 SYSEVAL and the HP-28 will find the text string "XYZ" and will bring

it back to level 1. If you have an HP-28C with extra memory or an
HP-28S then look in Appendix E to find what value to use instead of
#4FFF0.

Thus you can build up a text string which contains any characters
you like, and then use SYSEVAL to bring back a selected part of that
string to the stack, producing any kind of object you like. Let us
try to make a non-normalized number with an unusual sign, with a 0
in the most significant digit, and with a value B in the exponent.

A   00123444D432 B04

Sign not	Mantissa with	Exponent
0 or 9	leading zeros	with
	and digit D	digit B

The number would be stored internally back to front, with its
defining address in front of it:

3392040B234D44432100A

Now we can build up a text string which contains this string of
hexadecimal digits. First of all, we need to split this string of
hex digits into bytes, and the two digits (nybbles) of each byte
must be exchanged, because the HP-28 stores characters with their
nybbles back to front too. The string of bytes becomes:

#30 #93 #02 #04 #2B #43 #4D #44 #23 #01 #A0

The first byte has to be #3x, not #3, because each byte has two
nybbles in it, in reverse order, so 3 could not be used on its own.
I have used #30, but it could be anything else from #31 to #3F,
since the second digit will not be used. We can build up this
string using CHR (from the STRING menu) to create each character in
turn, but CHR expects real numbers, so let us turn the hexadecimal
numbers into real numbers:

48 147 2 4 43 67 77 68 35 1 160

Finally, we can build up the required text string; type 48 CHR to
put the first character of the text string in level 1, then 147 CHR
+ to make the next character and add it to the text string, then 2
CHR + and so on. Store this character string in a completely new

variable, such as NNN;   'NNN STO.

This new variable lies at the very top of memory and contains 21 nybbles which make up our Non-Normalized number (plus the spare nybble at the front), so the NNN begins 20 nybbles below the top of memory, at address #4FFEB. You can work this out using the HP-28 itself; #4FFFF-20 is #4FFEB. Set STD mode and do #4FFEB (see Appendix E if necessary) SYSEVAL. If you have followed the above instructions you will see the Non-Normalized number:

-0.01234445432E-696

It is immediately obvious that this an NNN because the exponent lies below the normal limit of -499. There are also two leading zeros, which would not be there in any normalized number displayed in STD mode. Creating this NNN took a lot of time; in future we shall use programs to make the job easier.

How does such an NNN behave, and what can you do with it? Press ENTER twice to make two more copies of the number, and type ABS CHS to get the number with a minus sign; this looks just like the copy in level 2, but if you try == then you will see the two numbers are not equal, because the lower one had a real minus sign while the upper one had its sign given by the hexadecimal digit A. DROP the zero, press ENTER and CHS; the number will keep its minus sign, because CHS expects to work only with signs given by 0 or 9. Press ABS to get the true positive value, and press LOG - you will see the log correctly given as -697.908528103, so the LOG function can correctly work with NNNs like this, though of course trying ALOG will just give zero or an UNDERFLOW error. DROP the result and ENTER to make another copy, then press #30B7 SYSEVAL (this is the main part of BIP) and check with ERRN to see that the error number is #32B04 - this confirms that the exponent now contains a digit other than 0 to 9, which shows that you can now use NNNs to check all possible error messages.

Now we come to the original point of all this - creating a name with a plus sign in it. You may have noticed that the text string we made a while ago had +CMD in the middle; this is the correct name for the subprogram which we wrote in section 3.7 to enable the command stack. DROP the error number and write the program << #7786 SYSEVAL >>, then SWAP and use the generalized STO program to create a variable containing the program and having the name '+CMD'. Use 'Sto' if you still have that program or simply do #3FBA7 SYSEVAL. You will find you have made your very own "customized" +CMD command.

3.10 Non-Normalized objects, and a programmable CONT and SST. The process used above to make a Non-Normalized number was very slow; it can be speeded up a lot if you have a program to do most of the job for you. Once the program is written, you will be able to use it to build up a text string which contains any object you want, not just a Non-Normalized number. Then you would use SYSEVAL to extract your Non-Normalized object from the string. Instead of using Non-Normalized numbers and the generalized STO, you could for example directly create a name containing characters that are normally not allowed inside a name. Such a name could be put on the stack, or stored in another variable, and then it could be used to create a variable with that name, to VISIT that variable, or to PURGE it. In this section I shall first show what programs are needed, then I shall use them to build up a variable which provides a programmable CONT. On the HP-41 CONT is called R/S; this name cannot be created on the HP-28 by normal means, but the programs shown below will let you create the name.

As shown in the previous point, the first thing to do is to write out your object as a string of hexadecimal characters. This cannot be automated very far; it is up to the user to decide what non-normalized object to create.

You must then type the string into the HP-28, and make sure it is correct. The next thing is to make sure the string written this way contains an even number of characters, since it will later be turned into a string of bytes, and each byte is made up of two hexadecimal characters. Here is a program to make sure a string contains an even number of characters:

```
<< IF DUP SIZE 2 MOD THEN "0"
   SWAP + END >> 'EVEN' STO
```

The program duplicates the string in level 1, finds its length, and finds the remainder of the length divided by 2. If the remainder is 1 then the length is odd, so the THEN part of the program puts a "0" at the front of the string, to make its length even. Try typing "ABC" and pressing EVEN; the result will be "0ABC" which now has an even number of characters. If you press EVEN again then nothing more will happen, as the string has an even number of characters.

The text string can now be turned into bytes - two characters at a time must be taken from the front of the string and turned into a byte. As was pointed out previously, the two characters must be placed in reverse order. Thus the string "0ABC" must have its first two characters removed and turned into the single byte whose value is 0A. Here is a program "FBYTE" which turns the first two characters of a string into a byte, and leaves the rest of the string in level 2:

Program lines	Explanation
`<< DUP 3 OVER SIZE SUB`	;Save a copy with all except the ;first 2 chars.
`"#" ROT 1 2 SUB +`	;Turn the first two chars xy into ;string "#xy"
`RCLF 8 STWS HEX`	;Save flag status, set word size 8 and ;HEX mode
`SWAP STR->`	;Get "#xy" and turn it into binary ;number #xy
`RR RR RR RR B->R CHR`	;Turn #xy into #yx, then real number, ;then char
`SWAP STOF >>`	;Replace original flags and modes. ;(Remember to do this yourself if the ;program fails!)
`'FBYTE' STO`	;Store this as a program called FBYTE

Set up this program, then make sure "0ABC" is in level 1, and press FBYTE. You will find an odd character in level 1; this is #A0 expressed as a byte, and the rest of the string "BC" will be left in level 2. The program sets HEX mode so as to make sure that the string "#xy" will be converted into a binary integer correctly, and a wordsize of 8 is set so that four rotations to the right will have the effect of swapping the two nybbles of the number - four rotations to the left would have just the same result.

The two programs EVEN and FBYTE can now be used as subprograms in a program which takes a whole "source" string of hexadecimal characters and turns it into a "result" string of bytes:

```
<<  EVEN                    ;Make sure source string length is even
    ""  SWAP                ;Put result string, initially empty,
                            ;in level 2
    WHILE  DUP  SIZE        ;Keep going while source string length
    REPEAT                  ;not zero
    FBYTE  ROT  SWAP  +     ;Get byte and add to result string
    SWAP
    END  DROP  >>           ;When finished drop empty source string


'COD'  STO                  ;Store this as a program called COD;
                            ;"code"
```

To see how this works, use it to create a result string which contains the letters "PQR". These letters are represented in ASCII by the hexadecimal bytes 50, 51, 52. Since the HP-28 reverses the two hexadecimal characters in each byte, we shall have to write these ASCII bytes as 051525. Type the source string "051525, then press COD. If you do not see the result string "PQR" in level 1 then check the programs you have entered from the above instructions and correct any mistakes.

You can use COD to turn any source string which gives a list of hexadecimal digits into a result string which expresses the same hexadecimal digits as a string of bytes. You could use this, for instance, to create strings of characters to control the printer and use it for graphics. Our purpose here is to use COD to create a string which can then be turned into a non-normalized object, so let us write one more program to do that:

```
<< 327680  R->B     ;Calculate the position where the result
   OVER  SIZE  -     ;string will begin in memory
   SWAP  COD         ;Create the result string
   'NNO'  DUP        ;Store result in 'NNO', but first purge any
   PURGE  STO        ;other variable with this name, so result will
                     ;be at the top of memory (PURGE gives no error
   SYSEVAL  >>       ;if NNO does not exist) SYSEVAL evaluates the
                     ;object and brings it to level 1.


'NNC'  STO           ;Store the program "Non-Normalized Create"
```

As in the last point, we know that the top of memory is at #4FFFF, which is 327679 in decimal. If we subtract the object length from this number + 1 then we have the address where the object begins. This must be calculated before the string is turned into an even number of hexadecimal digits, since we are interested in knowing where the object begins, regardless of the need for an extra digit which only rounds the string to an even length. I use the real number 327680 in preference to #50000 in case the program is accidentally typed in on an HP-28C set to DEC or OCT mode. On an HP-28S you would avoid this problem by typing #50000h regardless of the mode. In any case, if you have an HP-28S, or should you add some extra memory to an HP-28C, then the top of memory will not be at #4FFFF - you will have to replace #4FFFF (or 327679) and #50000 (or 327680) here and elsewhere by the position of the top of memory in your HP-28; Appendix E gives details.

Here is a use for NNC. If you put HALT in a program, it stops and waits for you to carry on one step at a time with SST, or to let the program continue running by pressing CONT. If you often stop programs to ask questions, it can become very tiresome pressing SHIFT 1 to let the program continue. The HP-41 had a key called R/S (for Run/Stop) at the bottom right-hand corner. You could press this key to restart a program just by touch - no need to press SHIFT or to hunt around on the keyboard. People who have used an HP-41, and others, may prefer to have an R/S key in the menu, preferably at the right hand end, so as to be able to press a single easily located key to let a program continue. It is also annoying to have to move to the Program Control menu so as to use SST. Let us put both in the USER menu, with suitable labels.

The SYSEVAL address for SST is #105BC, so you can write the program:

<< # 105BC SYSEVAL >>

and store it with the name SST (or Sst). Then you can HALT a program and press SST in the USER menu to single step through your program. (Again, remember to check Appendix E if you have a newer HP-28C or an HP-28S.)

Similarly the SYSEVAL address for CONT is #1058A, so you can write the program << # 1058A SYSEVAL >> and assign it to a menu key, then press that key to restart a program after it has been stopped by HALT. HP-41 users will want to call that key R/S, but 'R/S' will be interpreted by the HP-28 as an algebraic expression, not as a name.

The name 'R/S' can be written in ASCII as 522F53. To write it as a name stored in the HP-28 we must put its defining address in front, then its length, and reverse the length and the ASCII characters. This makes: 21D203025F235. Put the program << # 1058A SYSEVAL >> in level 2 of the stack, and the string "21D203025F235" in level 1, then press the NNC key. You will have to wait a short while, because NNC does a fair amount of work, then you will see the name 'R/S' in level 1 of the stack. You can simply press STO to store the program with this name, but it would be wise to make a duplicate copy of the name and store it in another variable before creating the variable R/S itself.

You need to keep a copy of the name because it is a "non-normalized" name. This means that when you want to PURGE it, or RCL or VISIT or

ORDER it, you will not be able to type in the name from the keyboard. Neither will you be able to get the name by pressing the single quote key and the menu key marked R/S. Both operations just put the characters that make up the name into the command line. Remember that the characters in the command line are "compiled" into an object only when the command line is evaluated - and the characters 'R/S will be compiled into an algebraic expression because they begin with ' and include /. Thus if you want to use the name R/S, you will have to fetch it from the stack or from a named variable.

It might seem just as easy to recreate the name R/S again if you need it later, using the program NNC as just shown above. Unfortunately, this does not work. Once a name refers to a variable that exists, a program will automatically evaluate that name when it is found. This means that if you use NNC to create the name again then the name will indeed be created, but NNC will not fetch it to the stack, instead it will execute the program called R/S. To create a non-normalized name and bring it to the stack again after a variable with that name has been created, you need to fetch the name from a program which contains the name in its quoted form. This means you have to use NNC to create the program << 'R/S' >> and to evaluate it. That might not seem too bad but the program looks like this:

Command	Hexadecimal code	Meaning
	7C620	Prepare to begin a program
<<	A0F72	Initialize program
	43F72	The following name is quoted
	21D20	The following is a name
	30	The name has three characters
R/S'	25F235	The character values (no symbol needed for ' at end)
>>	E4F72	Program finishes
	F1F72	Tidy up after program
	09F20	Object ends, can go on to evaluate next object

If you are so inclined, and if there is enough memory left in your HP-28C, you can try typing in all the code from the second column as one long text string, then pressing NNC, and you will get the name 'R/S' in level 1 of the stack after a suitable wait. Each of the hexadecimal codes represents either an internal HP-28 subprogram which does a specific job, or a command, or a stack object. All of these have to be entered back to front, as given above; as usual the addresses apply to version 1BB of the HP-28C.

These examples should give you an idea of what can be done with Non-Normalized objects. If you have the time, you may want to experiment further. Some of these programs will be used again in the next chapter.

3.11 Program control of menus. Another useful operation would be to select and control menus from within programs. If you have more than six variables you may want to use a program which HALTs to ask questions whose answers can be obtained by use of other programs from the hidden part of the USER menu. Again, you might have six commonly used programs in the first part of the USER menu, and then the second part could contain your customized SST and R/S. In either case, you can use << #E514 SYSEVAL CLMF >> to provide a NEXT program. Then you can use this in other programs to go from one part of the USER menu to the next, or the one after, and so on back to the first one. The newly selected menu does not appear until the program HALTs or finishes, but that is no problem as this is when you need to see the menu. Remember the naming rules given in 2.14; call this program 'NXT' or 'Next'. An additional use for it will be described in point 5.10.

If you want to select some other menu from a program then you need a more complicated operation (unless you have an HP-28S). << #E38E SYSEVAL >> works to select a menu, but this expects the menu number to be given in level 1 of the stack. The menu number is not given by a real number or a binary integer; it is given by an object called an "integer". An integer is a number stored with just five digits and no exponent, such objects are not available to the user of the HP-28, but they are provided by the operating system and are used internally by the HP-28. Objects of this type are available on the HP-71B, and the name "integer" is used on the HP-28 by analogy with the HP-71B. (The HP-28 designers may have another name, but we won't know what it is unless they tell us.) To get an integer to the stack, we use SYSEVAL (what else?). Since integers are used a lot by the operating system, the HP-28 provides SYSEVAL addresses which put any of the integers from 0 to 43 onto the stack. The integer 0 is given by #6D56 SYSEVAL, 1 is given by #6D60, and so on every ten nybbles. Thus you can write a program to get any integer from 0 to 43 onto the stack:

<< 10 * #6D56 + SYSEVAL >> 'INTR' STO

Put a real number between 0 and 43 on the stack, and press INTR to get the equivalent integer. You will see the integer displayed as "System Object". That is the name used to represent any object which is not recognized by the instructions used to set up the display, you might have come across it already if you have been playing with SYSEVAL or have been unlucky enough to meet one of the HP-28's few "bugs". In fact the stack itself contains only the addresses of objects, and most such addresses are recognized by the instructions which "decompile" and display them, but if you get an address which has no associated display information then the display shows System Object instead. Thus a System Object is really any address not recognized as an object or a command, and this is related to the cryptic explanation of SYSEVAL in the Manuals. That explanation says SYSEVAL "evaluates the system object" at the address given to SYSEVAL. In fact this means that SYSEVAL evaluates the program given by the address given to it, and any address at all can be considered a system object - SYSEVAL will just go to that address and try to use it as a program, regardless of what is really there. SYSEVAL actually reads the number at the address given to it, and uses that number as the address of a program to be run - thus any address containing 0 makes SYSEVAL jump on to address #0 of the HP-28, which is the address of the System Halt instructions; this is why SYSEVAL so often has the effect of clearing the stack and display - it is resetting the HP-28 according to the System

Halt. Most other addresses cause SYSEVAL to bring some random address to the stack, and this is why so many attempts to use SYSEVAL display "System Object".

You might like to change the program so it does not try to create integers above 43. Let's get back to menus, their numbers on the HP-28C are listed below; we shall see how a MENU command can be written to select them. On an HP-28S the numbers are different but it has a built-in MENU command anyway.

0	Cursor menu, menu line cleared.	16	STORE	
		17	PRINT	
1	USER	18	ARRAY	
2	SOLV	19	CMPLX	
3	Program Branch	20	STRING	
4	LOGS	21	PLOT	
5	STAT	22	Initial FORM submenu	
6	MODE	23	DNEG	etc. FORM submenu
7	TRIG	24	-(), <-->	etc. FORM submenu
8	STACK	25	AF	FORM submenu
9	ALGEBRA	26	1/(), <-->	etc. FORM submenu
10	SOLV (again)	27	-(), L()	etc. FORM submenu
11	BINARY	28	1/(), E()	etc. FORM submenu
12	LIST	29	1/(), E^	etc. FORM submenu
13	REAL	30	-(), L*	etc. FORM submenu
14	Program Control	31	->()	FORM submenu
15	Program Test			

An awkward feature of the HP-28 is that you cannot easily use the left-hand keyboard while holding the HP-28 in one hand. If you have the HP-28 in one hand, with the left-hand keyboard folded under, then you can use the right hand keyboard including the menus, but you have to turn the whole thing over to get at the other keyboard. Once you have turned over the HP-28, you can spell out a command, or select a menu, or select the CATALOG, then you can go back to the right-hand menu and carry on. The SYSEVAL addresses described above can let you write an HP-28C MENU program which you can use from the

USER menu to select any other menu, without turning the HP-28C over. That means you can use the HP-28C much more like an HP-41 or any other truly handheld vertical format calculator. (On an HP-28S you need only write a program which puts the built-in MENU command in the USER menu.) Here is a general HP-28C MENU command:

<< 10 * #6D56 + SYSEVAL
#E38E SYSEVAL CLMF >> 'MENU' STO

To select any of the menus given in the list above, put the menu number in level 1 and press MENU, or use it from within a program. Since menus are normally selected from the keyboard, the instructions within #E38E do not reset the display, as that is normally done after any keyboard command. This means that the MENU program has to contain CLMF to force the display to be reset. Note that only the first section of each menu is selected by this program, you can use NEXT from the keyboard or from within a program (see above) to select other parts of a menu. Menus 22 to 31 expect a special form of algebraic expression in the display, so they should not be activated from within a program, but all the others can be fetched with MENU. If you like the idea of using MENU to select menus without needing the lefthand keyboard then you could glue a label with a list of menu numbers on the space above the HP-28C display (you can this on an HP-28S too but it needs different numbers). This label would not need to have all menu numbers, only those of menus on the lefthand keyboard. In fact there should still be room on it for a list of the flags which control modes.

If you only want to select a few menus then you could write programs to select individual menus, with the address of the relevant integer (#6D6A for 2 and so on) included directly in each program.

3.12 A NAME command. Some FORTH dialects provide the command NAME which takes the <u>address</u> of a command from the stack and replaces it with the <u>name</u> of that variable. Steen Petersen has discovered a similar command on the HP-28C:

<< #30064 SYSEVAL >> 'NAME STO

creates the command NAME. Now go to the USER menu and press a key which brings any user variable to the stack, or use RCL to bring a variable to the stack. Then press NAME and the displayed variable will be replaced by a text string giving its name. If you still have the variable G (created in point 2.1; put it in again if you want to try the following) in the USER menu then press G and you will see 6.67E-11. Now press NAME and this will be replaced by "G", the name of the variable. If the object in level 1 is <u>not</u> a variable but a stack object then NAME returns a null string (except for the numbers -5,-4,-3,-2,-1,0, 8, 9 which all return meaningless text strings). This program will let you check whether an item on the stack is stored in a variable, for example to see if a command is a built-in HP-28 command or one written by the user. The main interest of NAME, however, is in that it tells us that the stack contains not the variables themselves, but only their addresses, since this is what allows a variable to be replaced by its name.

3.13 Using EDIT in your programs. You can activate EDIT by doing #C407 SYSEVAL. This drops #C407 from the stack, activates the cursor menu, and puts the object that is now in level 1 onto the bottom line of the display. If a program is not running then you can do exactly the same by pressing EDIT, so the only saving provided by an EDIT program is that you will not need to press SHIFT. If a program is running then that program carries on running until it comes to its end or until HALT is encountered. Only then is the object which was in level 1 displayed in inverse (white on black) and the HP-28 waits for you to edit it. This means that a program can put different objects in the command line and in level 1 of the stack. If you press ENTER then the object in the command line replaces that in level 1, if you press ATTN then the object in level 1 stays there and the command line is removed.

You can use ....#C407 SYSEVAL.... in a program to invite the user to edit an object, then press ENTER, and then CONT (or R/S from earlier in this chapter) to carry on a program. Because it behaves as described above, you can also use this SYSEVAL address to give a user a choice of two answers to a question. Say you want to ask whether the positive or negative square root of a number is wanted.

You could write the following piece of program:

    ....SQRT "+ve or -ve root?" 1 #C407

      SYSEVAL NEG HALT SWAP DROP *....

If you press ATTN and CONT then the program drops the message and multiplies the square root by -1, if you press ENTER and CONT then you get the positive square root.

* * *

That is quite enough for one chapter. The next one will tell you something about machine language programming, but it also gives more details of SYSEVAL, so it is worth reading even if you are not that keen on machine language programming itself.

CHAPTER 4 – MACHINE LANGUAGE PROGRAMMING

To get the greatest control possible over any computer (and this includes calculators) you have to program that computer in its machine language. Various names are given to machine languages, and there are various approaches to writing machine language programs, but the fundamental aim is to produce a string of numbers, each of which activates part of the Central Processor Unit (CPU) making it do something rather simple. All programs and programming languages are ultimately built up from instructions ("code") in machine language. To obtain full control of the HP-28 you must program it in machine language, but to do that you need to know more about the layout of the HP-28, about the structure of programs, and how to tell the HP-28 that something is a piece of machine language code. This book does not cover all details of machine language programming, but it will give some details and some examples. The first few points of this chapter will lay the groundwork. I shall use version 1BB addresses in the examples, remember to check Appendix E if you have a different version of the HP-28.

4.1 The layout of programs. The simple program NIP shown in point 2.5 was:

<< SWAP DROP >>. This can be interpreted as follows:

<<	SWAP	DROP	>>
Begin	Do the	Do the	Finish
a ---then---	SWAP ---then---	DROP ---then---	a
program	command	command	program

This looks quite simple, say like beads one after another on a string. Now look at the program in point 2.5 which uses NIP:

```
<<          +        LAST                    NIP              >>

Begin              Fetch                              Finish the
  a    --add--   arguments                               main
Program          used by +    \                     /   program
                          fall through to      return to
                          subprogram NIP    main program
                                  \                 /
                          << -- SWAP -- DROP -- >>
```

The string has an extra thread in it now. If NIP were to use
another subprogram then there would be yet another thread. If
another subprogram was used between + and LAST there would be
another thread too. Nevertheless, you would still be able to draw a
"string" which would track one command after another through the
program. (OK, I am ignoring loops, but that's just an added
complication - you could write out each execution of the loop one
after another and still have a continuous string.) But actually the
string follows an even more complicated route, after all each
command is itself made up of simpler subprograms. Let us follow NIP
again, and concentrate on what SWAP does in more detail:

```
<< --                     SWAP                   -- DROP -- >>
    \                                          /
     begin a   ---  check if  ---  swap the --- finish the
     subprogram     there are      object       subprogram
                    at least 2     addresses
                    objects on     around on
                    the stack      the stack
```

Now we have reached the lowest level, each of the "beads" on this
"string" is a short(ish) subprogram written in machine language.
Each of these machine language subprograms finishes with three
instructions which let the HP-28 jump to the next subprogram on the
string. Let us go back and see how the HP-28 keeps track of where
it is on this string. The program NIP is actually stored as the
addresses of the subprograms that make it up:

	<<	SWAP	DROP	>>	
02C67	27F0A	17825	1783F	27F1F	02F90
begin a	start a	do SWAP	do DROP	end a	finish
subprogram	user program			user program	subprogram

The instructions at the address 02C67 are an actual machine language program which says "hang on, what follows is not going to be machine code yet, it's going to be another subprogram made up of a list of addresses". The instructions at 27F0A make sure the HP-28 knows that what follows is a program written by the user, not a subprogram built into the HP-28 operating system. The instructions at address 17825 look like:

02C67	1C3A5	120F5	02F90
begin a	check at	do a	finish
subprogram	least 2	SWAP	subprogram
	objects		

The instructions at 02C67 are once again used to say "what follows is a list of addresses". The instructions at 1C3A5 and at 120F5 both point to subprograms in machine code, and the instructions at 02F90 are machine code which takes you back up one level of subprogram. Let us look at the sort of program that would be stored at 120F5 - this can serve as an example of a machine language subprogram. The first column below gives the address of each step (instruction), the second column is the hexadecimal number which is that instruction, the third column is the Saturn "mnemonic" for that instruction, the fourth column briefly explains what that instruction does.

address (hex)	contents (hex)	equivalent instruction	explanation
120F5	120FA	REL(5) 5	address where machine code begins
120FA	143	A=DAT1 A	copy data pointed to by D1 (level 1) to A

120FD	174	D1=D1+ 5	move pointer up by 5 to point at level 2
12100	147	C=DAT1 A	copy data pointed to by D1 (level 2) to C
12103	141	DAT1=A A	copy A to level 2(pointed to by D1)
12106	1C4	D1=D1- 5	move pointer to point at level 1
12109	145	DAT1=C	copy C to level 1(pointed to by D1)
1210C	142	A=DAT0 A	copy data pointed to by D0 into A D0 actually points to the address where the address of the next instruction is held - in this case it is 02F90 which is the next address after 120F5 in the list
1210F	164	D0=D0+ 5	add 5 to D0 so it will point to the next address on the thread after this one - in fact this will be changed since we have reached the end of this subprogram
12112	808C	PC=(A)	jump to the address given by the address in A; don't go to 02F90 itself but to the address given by the contents of 02F90

If you already know about machine language programming on the HP-71B or on other CPUs then you should be able to follow the above without too much trouble, otherwise don't worry too much if it does not all make sense yet. The instruction 808C is called PC=(A) and is a new instruction used by the modified Saturn CPU which is in the HP-28. This instruction lets a program jump from one set of instructions to the next by using indirect addressing (a common machine code method). Because this instruction is used to move from one piece of machine code to the next, each piece of machine code that is reached this way must have its address stored somewhere, usually just in front of that code. In this example 120F5 is stored as the address which tells how the SWAP code can be found, and at 120F5 we find 120FA which is the address where the machine code actually begins, in this case immediately following 120F5.

Note that this example of machine code just swaps round two values. These are not two objects on the stack; they are the addresses of two stack objects. In other words the stack itself is just a list of addresses, each of which points to an object. This same piece of code shows that the pointer D1 usually points to the lowest level address of the stack, in other words to the address which gives the address of the level 1 object. The pointer D0 points to the address which will be used for the next step of the present program or subprogram. Whenever a subprogram begins, the previous contents of D0 must be saved in a "return stack", and D0 must be filled with the first address of the new subprogram (thread), that is what the instructions at 02C67 do. When a subprogram (thread) finishes, the instructions at 02F90 bring back the previous value of D0 from the return stack so that the program which called this subprogram can itself carry on.

Now for a little history! To learn how to write HP-28 machine language programs it was necessary to recognize that a machine code program could be written by starting it with the address of the first instruction and by ending it with the three instructions that continue the thread. Some people, particularly at HP, may wonder how this was discovered. Let me assure the HP folks that no one at HP gave away the secret! To discover it I first used Ianization to find the addresses of all the standard commands in the CATALOG. That showed most commands were separated from the next command by $N*5 + 1$ nybbles, but a few had some other separation. This suggested most commands were made up of a string of subprogram addresses, plus one (or six) nybbles to identify the command, but that a few commands had pieces of machine code embedded in them. Then I used a rather tedious procedure using another useful SYSEVAL address (which I discovered in the top 2K of the ROM whose examination I had shared with Ian Maw). This allows the length of a variable to be changed, so that the next variable in the USER menu appears to begin at a different address than it really does. I could thus make variables appear to be made up of instructions which were really part of the ROM. Then I could use Ianization to turn these variables into new variable names, and thus bring them to the command line.

Once the "name" was in the command line I could analyze it with NUM, and thus find what the code was in the unusual commands. Some of the code was indeed not made up of addresses but I could interpret it as machine language instructions, using the list of Saturn instruction codes given in the HP-71B Internal Documentation Set. After checking two or three pieces of machine code I recognized the addresses at the beginning and the code at the end - the number 808C is not described in the HP-71B IDS, but Bill Wickes in an article about the HP-28 had mentioned the new PC=(A) instruction and its use, so it seemed clear that 808C was PC=(A) being used to jump to the next command. These discoveries provided me with enough information to write a PEEK function (see section 4.4) and from there on it was possible to study the HP-28 and learn the many things described here.

A language which carries out higher-level commands as pieces of machine code and follows a string, or "thread", as has been described is called a threaded language, or a threaded interpreter. The language provided to the users, with commands such as << or DROP or SWAP, is a threaded language. The same commands are used within commands; as we have seen, the SWAP command itself is made up of a list of addresses. This language is called RPL by the people who designed the HP-18, HP-19 and HP-28 - a subset of RPL is available to the normal user of the HP-18, HP-19 or HP-28, and a larger subset of it is made available by SYSEVAL. The whole language has still more commands, some of which are not needed in the HP-28, so they have not been included. What does RPL stand for? Well, the design team themselves do not seem to have been too sure! It is a name very similar to RPN (Reverse Polish Notation) which was the name for the notation used by previous HP calculators. RPL is reputed to stand for "Reverse Polish LISP", which shows its origins in RPN, and also its affinity to LISP which is a computer language that uses lists and local variables (called "lambda variables" in

LISP). Another suggestion is that RPL could stand for "ROM-based Procedural Language". Anyhow, the design team says "Ripple" without worrying too much what it stands for. If you look at my name you will understand why I like to call it Reverse Polish Language!

4.2 Copyrights and copy wrongs. The operating system of the HP-28 is a valuable piece of programming and is protected by Hewlett Packard copyrights. This means that it is wrong to copy it or publish it, and in the examples above I have not used the actual code from the HP-28 operating system. Instead I have written some similar code which could do the same thing - it shows how a simple machine code program looks and how it is executed. To write your own machine code programs you need to know a few more things, including the instructions and registers used by the Saturn CPU. That information is published in the HP-71B IDS which are also copyright, so I cannot simply copy that information here. Appendix D provides a short summary, and information on the subject has been published in user club journals too, but to have a full description you should get a copy of either Volume I of the HP-71B Software IDS, or the Hardware Specifications volume of the IDS. The former is cheaper, at a mere $50 or thereabouts. If you are a member of a user club you might be able to borrow a copy from the club library or from one of the members who use an HP-71B and have a copy. The information provided in Appendix D and in the examples in this chapter will give you enough information to get started in machine language programming, but it will not cover all the instructions.

Most people who write machine language programs do not actually write out strings of numeric instructions. Instead they use "mnemonics" which are short alphabetic names for each instruction. These mnemonics are then translated into a string of numbers by a program called an "assembler". This simplifies machine language programming considerably because human beings usually find names much easier to remember than numbers. Assemblers often simplify machine language programming further by letting programmers use label names (to mark places in programs) and other symbols, for example a symbol which means "the address of this instruction". Assemblers also provide instructions which are not translated directly into a number to specify a machine language operation, but which create a constant to be used by an instruction, or which help control information printed by the assembler. Such instructions are often called pseudo-operations, or just pseudo-ops. The first instruction in the example machine code program for SWAP is such a pseudo-op; it does not create an instruction, instead it provides the five-nybble number which represents the address 5 nybbles forward RELative to the current address. Assemblers which let people write machine language programs for the Saturn CPU are used by Hewlett Packard on their own computers, and have also been written for use on IBM PCs and compatible computers running under MS-DOS. HP also sell a plug-in module for the HP-71B which includes a FORTH language translator and a Saturn assembler. Assemblers for the Saturn have been written by members of HP user clubs, these include the "AREUH" Development System for the HP-71B written by Pierre David and Janick Taillandier of the Paris club and the "Turbo-71" assembler written by Stefano Tendon of the Italian user club.

A program written as a list of mnemonics and pseudo-ops is often called an assembly language program - it is written in a language which the assembler recognizes and turns into a string of numerical machine language instructions. Consequently the names "assembly language" and "machine language" are often used as if they meant exactly the same thing, and as both are related to the simple individual instructions used by the CPU they are called low-level languages. Both types of language are different from higher level languages which are usually "compiled" or "interpreted" or both. An RPL program written by a user is a string of letters, numbers and special symbols typed in on the command line; even the names on menu keys are put in as the characters which make up the name. After ENTER is pressed, the HP-28 "compiles" this string and turns it into a program made up of, and stored as, individual command addresses and objects. When such a program is "run" or "executed", each command address is "interpreted" and executed as a set of lower-level commands or machine language instructions. When an object or program has to be displayed, printed or edited, the HP-28 goes through the commands and objects, and "decompiles" them, producing a string of letters and other characters again so that the user can recognize them. This business of decompiling objects and programs is complicated and therefore slow, which is why the HP-28 display can take a (relatively) long time to catch up with what you are doing. This is all the more noticeable because the HP-28 has a four-line display. In order to speed things up a little, and to save some space in memory, long objects are not decompiled completely, only that part which needs to be put in the display is decompiled, but even this can be slow. If an address cannot be recognized as a command or an object then the HP-28 decompiler puts the words "System Object" in its place. Clearly, you cannot compile these words again, they do not stand for a unique command or object which can be put in their place, so it is not possible successfully to edit a program, variable, or stack object which contains the words "System Object". The words are compiled as two unquoted names: System and Object, and if you try to evaluate them or run a program which contains them then the HP-28 puts them onto the stack as unevaluated quoted names. Then you can really confuse matters if you create variables called 'System' or 'Object' and the HP-28 tries to use them!

The manual for the HP-71B FORTH/Assembler module can be of some help to people wanting to write machine language programs for the HP-28 - it describes the Saturn CPU and the instructions it uses, but does not give the numbers that represent each instruction. Now, the HP-28C has too little RAM to hold an assembler, so anyone wanting to write their own machine language programs has to type the programs in directly in the form of numbers (though the HP-28S has enough RAM typing an assembler program in would still be very time-consuming). If you have an assembler on a PC or on the HP-71B then you can write a program in mnemonics, assemble it on the PC or 71, then type the numbers into the HP-28C. Otherwise, you have to do the assembly by hand, writing out the program number by number. This is not much trouble for short programs, but can be very laborious if you decide to write a long program. The best thing to do on an HP-28 is write a mini-assembler which takes a string of hexadecimal digits and turns them into a program that the HP-28 will recognize. This works much like the COD program in the previous chapter, we shall come to it soon.

The opposite to an assembler is a "disassembler" - a program which reads a string of numbers and prints out the mnemonics which represent the program which the numbers provide. Once again, entering a disassembler is too long for comfort, but a mini-disassembler can be written to read a piece of code from the HP-28 RAM or ROM and to translate it into a string of hexadecimal digits. Then you can type those digits into a bigger computer and disassemble them properly, or you can try to disassemble them by hand, comparing the numbers with a list of Saturn instruction codes.

The FORTH/Assembler module also provides a FORTH language interpreter for the HP-71B. FORTH is in many ways similar to the RPN used by earlier HP calculators, it uses a threaded interpreter, and HP-28 RPL is in many ways similar to FORTH on the HP-71B. For example the HP-71B FORTH language uses the pointer D0 as an instruction pointer, and pointer D1 as a data-stack pointer, in just the same way as was explained above in the description of SWAP. Thus the manual for the FORTH/Assembler module is another possible source of information for someone trying to understand the HP-28.

Enough about sources of information! More are listed in Appendix A, let us now see how you can write a machine language program on your HP-28.

4.3 A simple machine language program. There is more than one way to write and run a machine language program. In this point I shall begin with a very simple program and a simple method of putting it into the HP-28. The simplest possible program would have just one instruction, here I shall show a program which carries out the one machine language instruction INTOFF. This instruction disables all the keys except the ON/ATTN key.

As we saw in the example program in point 4.1, a machine language program begins with an address which points to the rest of the program, and it ends with the three instructions which point to the next command. If the program is to be put at the top of RAM, finishing at address #4FFFF, then we can work out all the other addresses. The result will be as below - you can see that some mnemonics in the third column are followed by parameters; these are called instruction "modifiers" and are in hexadecimal notation.

address (hex)	contents (hex)	equivalent instruction	explanation
4FFED	4FFF2	REL(5) 5	address where machine code begins
4FFF2	808F	INTOFF	Disable keyboard interrupts
4FFF6	142	A=DAT0 A	copy data pointed to by D0 into A
4FFF9	164	D0=D0+ 5	add 5 to D0 to point to next cmd
4FFFC	808C	PC=(A)	jump to the address given by A

To turn this program into a string of bytes we can use COD from chapter 3. Moreover to turn it into a string of bytes and execute it we just need to translate it with COD, store it at the top of memory, and jump to the the beginning (4FFED). This is exactly what the program NNC does.

So, make sure you have the programs EVEN, FBYTE, COD and NNC in your HP-28; if necessary type them in again, then type in the string of instructions as shown below, then press NNC. The string of hexadecimal digits represents the instructions that make up the program shown above, with the address at the front turned around.

"2FFF4808F142164808C"

If you have done everything correctly, then after pressing NNC you will wait a few seconds for the string to be turned into bytes, the program will be carried out, and the busy annunciator will turn off. Now press any key except ON and nothing will happen; the key will be ignored. Press a few more keys - they will be ignored because the program has disabled the keyboard. After you press a few keys, the keyboard will begin to respond, or you can reset it with a system halt (ON UP). You have written and used a machine language program which does something that no HP-28 command does!

This subprogram can be useful if you want to run a program and prevent accidental key-pushes being stored in the key buffer and read later on by the program. To run it again, you can do #4FFED SYSEVAL. This will only work if the program is in its place at the top of memory. You could do this with the following program which uses RCL to recall NNO to the stack, then PURGEs it, then STOs it again, then uses #4FFED SYSEVAL to execute it:

<< 'NNO' DUP RCL OVER
PURGE SWAP STO #4FFED SYSEVAL >>

This seems complicated: later on we shall see some other ways to store and execute machine code programs. If you want another program which enables the keyboard again then you will need to write a second machine language program which executes the instruction INTON - the code for this instruction is 8080, repeat the above process with 8080 replacing 808F. Clearly this program is no use in keyboard operations - either the keyboard is still disabled so you cannot use a menu key to re-enable it, or the keyboard has already been re-enabled in which case you no longer need to re-enable it. The program is useful though if you want to re-enable the keyboard before prompting for some input during a program.

The instructions to go to the next command on the thread are "142164808C", which is 10 nybbles long. These 10 nybbles could be stored in one place in ROM and all commands could end with a 7 nybble GOVLNG instruction (Go Very Long - go to another address anywhere in the whole memory) to go to those 10 nybbles and execute them. There must be about a thousand pieces of code which finish with these instructions, so this would save about one and a half thousand bytes of memory. If the 10 nybbles were stored in four or five places in ROM then all other commands could end with a GOLONG to the nearest place, and each GOLONG command would be 6 nybbles long, saving up to 2K bytes. It seems odd that the designers chose not to use this method but to finish every command with the same 10 nybbles. This saves a little time, 14 or 15 machine cycles to be precise, per command ending, but the 2K lost this way could have been used to provide some very useful commands, such as a few proper clock functions. Maybe the design team really did consider it necessary to get the extra speed, or maybe they decided it was not worth the time and trouble to write a translator which would improve the operating system in this way. (The same thread ending is used in the HP-28S.) In the program above I use the 10 nybble method to avoid relying on a ROM address which might change in new versions of the HP-28.

The method described here can be used to write other short machine language programs. Note how COD was used as a mini-assembler to turn a string of hexadecimal digits into a string of machine code.

4.4 A PEEK command. Anyone who wants to make a serious study of a computer or to program it in machine language needs a command to read any selected piece of memory, ROM or RAM. In BASIC this command is called PEEK. This point describes an HP-28 PEEK command, written in machine language. PEEK commands can be written to read different amounts of information, and to return them to the stack in different forms. The PEEK shown here has been written to help search the HP-28 ROM for interesting command names and messages, so it reads 8 bytes (16 nybbles) at a time and returns them to the stack as a text string. As with the interrupt disable program, this one is written so it does not rely on pieces of code in the ROM, in order to make sure that this PEEK can be used not only on version 1BB of the HP-28, but also on future ones, again see Appendix E for details.

First, here is a machine language program to read a piece of memory beginning at address xxxxx and to put it into a known place. That known place is address 4FFFF0, the very top of memory (on an unexpanded HP-28C). As in the previous point, instruction modifiers are in hexadecimal.

address (hex)	contents (hex)	equivalent instruction	explanation
?????	?????	REL(5) 5	address where machine code begins
?????	133	AD1EX	exchange A with D1 to save pointer
?????	103	R3=A	save A (old D1) in scratch R3
?????	1Fxxxxx	D1=xxxxx	set pointer D1 to required address
?????	15BF	A=DAT1l0	copy register pointed to by D1 into A
?????	1F0FFF4	D1=4FFF0	set pointer D1 to address 4FFF0
?????	159F	DAT1=Al0	copy register A to this address
?????	113	A=R3	recover pointer from R3
?????	131	D1=A	put original pointer value back in D1
?????	142	A=DAT0 A	get address of nxt command address
?????	164	D0=D0+ 5	add 5 to D0 to point to following command
?????	808C	PC=(A)	jump to the address given by A

We do not yet know the addresses at which the instructions will be stored, so the addresses have been written as ?????. If we store a text string of eight bytes in a variable at the very top of memory then this program will replace that "dummy" string with the value taken from the eight bytes beginning at address xxxxx. Some way has to be found though of putting that address into the program. The order of the nybbles that make up the address must not be changed, but the whole address must be put into the program back to front. One way to do this is to write xxxxx as a binary integer, since these are stored back to front, with the order of the nybbles unchanged. If the rest of the program is written as a binary integer too and the space for xxxxx is left filled with 00000 then it would be enough to OR the binary number xxxxx with the rest of the program to produce the required program. Since a binary integer can be a maximum of 16 nybbles long, and this program is more than 16 nybbles long, we cannot write the whole program as one binary integer, but we can write it as a list of four integers. Since each integer has an object definition and an object length stored in front of it, we must jump around the definitions and lengths to make up a program which is not affected by them. We still need to know where the program begins in memory so as to be able to jump to it with SYSEVAL, so the program is best placed as near the top of memory as possible, just below the dummy string. Let us use the name 'X1' for the list of binary numbers which contains the program, and the name 'X2' for the dummy string. The layout of the top of memory when we do this will be as shown below.

address (hex)	contents (hex)	equivalent instruction	explanation
4FF5F	20		length in bytes of object name 'X1'
4FF61	8513		object name 'X1' nybbles inverted
4FF65	20		length in bytes of name, again
4FF67	69A20		address of list definition
4FF6C	07A20		address defining first binary integer
4FF71	51000		length of binary integer+5 in nybbles

--------------- First binary integer begins below --------------------

address (hex)	contents (hex)	equivalent instruction	explanation
4FF76	B7FF4	REL(5) 5	address of program start
4FF7B	133	AD1EX	exchange A with D1 to save pointer
4FF7E	103	R3=A	save A (old D1) in scratch R3
4FF81	6E00	GOTO (*)+E	jump forward over intervening info
4FF85	0		fill out to end of binary integer

--------------- First binary integer finishes here --------------------

address (hex)	contents (hex)	equivalent instruction	explanation
4FF86	07A20		address defining second binary integer
4FF8B	51000		length, +5 to allow for length count

--------------- Second binary integer begins below --------------------

address (hex)	contents (hex)	equivalent instruction	explanation
4FF90	1F00000	D1=00000	set pointer D1 to required address
4FF97	15BF	A=DAT1 10	copy register pointed to by D1 into A
4FF9B	6E00	GOTO (*)+E	jump over intervening stuff again
4FF9F	B		fill out last nybble of binary integer

--------------- Second binary integer finishes here --------------------

4FFA0	07A20		address defining third binary integer
4FFA5	51000		length +5

--------------- Third binary integer begins here ----------------------

4FFAA	1F0FFF4	D1=4FFF0	set pointer D1 to address 4FFF0
4FFB1	159F	DAT1=A 10	copy register A to this address
4FFB5	6E00	GOTO (*)+E	jump over intervening stuff again
4FFB9	0		filler

--------------- Third binary integer ends here -----------------------

4FFBA	07A20		address defining 4th binary integer
4FFBF	51000		length +5

--------------- Fourth binary integer begins here --------------------

4FFC4	113	A=R3	recover pointer from R3
4FFC7	131	D1=A	put original pointer value back in D1
4FFCA	142	A=DAT0 A	get address of next command address
4FFCD	164	D0=D0+ 5	add 5 to D0 to point to following command
4FFD0	808C	PC=(A)	jump to the address given by A

--------------- Fourth and last binary integer of list ends here ------

4FFD4	09F20		address defining end of composite object
4FFD9	A7000		length in nybbles of name, object
4FFDE	20		length in bytes of object name 'X2'
4FFE0	8523		object name, 'X2'
4FFE4	20		length of name, again
4FFE6	E4A20		address defining a text string
4FFEB	51000		length+5 in nybbles
4FFF0	16-nybble dummy string		string to be replaced by PEEK result
			extends to top of memory at 4FFFF

This is long, but only needs to be written once. Let us now see
what the list of four binary integers looks like. Since they are to
be stored in the sequence given above they will have to be entered
in reverse order.

```
{          # E63013314FF7B
           # B00E6FB5100000F1
           # E6F9514FFF0F1
           # C808461241131311   }
```

Now we know what the binary list to be written looks like, we can write a program which creates this list, includes the address to be PEEKed in the second binary integer, then does the PEEK, extracts the result from X2 and puts it on the stack:

```
<<  RCWS  SWAP  28  STWS   ;Get original wordsize, set w-size to 28
    SLB  64  STWS          ;shift PEEK address one byte left, set
                           ;w-size 64
    # B00E6FB5100000F1  +  ;enter 2nd binary integer, add address
    # E63013314FF7B  SWAP  ;enter 1st binary integer & swap above
                           ;2nd
    # E6F9514FFF0F1        ;enter third binary integer
    # C808461241131311     ;enter fourth binary integer
    4  ->LIST              ;turn the 4 binary integers into a list
    'X1'  DUP  PURGE  STO  ;purge X1 and store list as X1
    "DUMMYSTR"             ;enter 8-character dummy string on stack
    'X2'  DUP  PURGE  STO  ;purge X2 and store string as X2
    # 4FF76  SYSEVAL       ;jump to program created inside the list
    STWS                   ;replace original word size
    X2  >>                 ;bring PEEKed string from X2 to stack


'PEEK'   STO              ;store the program
```

Now to see the contents of any address in memory, just put that address as a binary number in level 1 of the stack, and execute PEEK. The result comes back as a text string. Make doubly sure you have entered the program exactly as given (but if you have an HP-28 with more memory than a standard HP-28C then you should again remember to check Appendix E) and then test it out - for a start try #3FE7A PEEK - if you have a version 1BB HP-28C then you should see the text string "Version " which is the first part of the "Version 1BB" message displayed by #A SYSEVAL.

The program above uses several techniques which deserve to be explained before we set off PEEKing all over inside the HP-28. First of all, the user's original wordsize is saved on the stack, and later replaced. Secondly, a wordsize of 28 is set and the PEEK address is shifted left by one byte. We need to shift the address left by one byte so it will be added into the correct place in the binary integer #B00E6FB5100000F1 - the address must slot into the 00000 which is one byte to the left of the end of the number. By using a wordsize of 28 during the shift operation, the program truncates the shifted address to 28 bits long; a 20 bit address and 8 zero bits to its right. This means that if anyone accidentally tries to PEEK an address with more than 20 bits then only 20 bits will be used, so there is no chance of accidentally changing the program in the rest of the binary number. Now that the address has been shifted, the program sets a wordsize of 64 bits, so that none of the binary integers in the list will be changed, particularly during the addition of the address to its binary integer. OR would be just as good as + here, but + takes one less keystroke to type in.   The remaining binary integers are entered now; note that reading down their left hand side you get "BEEC" which sounds like PEEK, and serves as a reminder of what this program does, to differentiate it from the POKE program which will be introduced later and which looks very similar.   If you look back at the detailed listing of the binary program you will see that the first three binary integers all need an extra byte to fill them out at the end - in two cases this "filler" has been left as a zero, and therefore does not need to be typed in at all, but in the other one a B is used as a filler instead to produce this "BEEC".

Once the four binary numbers are ready and have been made into a list, the program tries to PURGE X2, in case there is a previous copy left which is not at the very top of memory. PURGE is a little unusual because it does not give an error if the variable it is trying to purge does not exist. This is helpful in cases such as this one, but it can be annoying if you mis-spell a variable name and therefore fail to purge it, without realizing this has happened.

PURGE has to behave somewhat like this though, because it can be used by a program to purge itself, so it cannot carry out the full purge operation till a program stops running, by which time it would be too late to complain if an error had occured. After the PURGE, the program stores the list in X1, securely placed at the top of memory. Then the program puts a dummy text string, 8 bytes long, on the stack, and repeats the purging and storing of X2. At this stage, everything is ready for the machine language program to be run - the program is next to top in the memory, and the dummy string is at the very top, ready to be replaced by the PEEKed string. The machine language program executes the operations described in the listing given earlier, reading 16 nybbles from the selected address, and putting them into X2, at address 4FFF0. Finally the program replaces the original wordsize, which has fallen to level 1 by now, and brings the PEEKed string to the stack by evaluating X2. If you need any more copies of the PEEKed value, you can bring them to the stack just by evaluating X2 again, even if X2 is moved away from the top of memory.

The binary program uses pointer D1 to pick up the PEEKed string from memory, but D1 is used as the stack pointer, so the program has to save the original contents of D1, and then to replace them. Subprograms which save and replace pointers do exist in the HP-28 operating system, but they might get moved to a different address in new versions, so I prefer to save the pointer without calling any subprograms from ROM. In the same way, I put the three instructions which finish a binary program into the program instead of going to some place in ROM whose address might change as well. By avoiding any reliance on subprograms in ROM, the program guarantees that it will work on future versions of the HP-28, so there will be no need to start all the deciphering of the operating system from scratch again. The only problem is that the position of the top of memory is not always the same, and that can be dealt with as described in Appendix E.

4.5 Playing with PEEK. Once you have a PEEK command you can go roaming around the memory of the HP-28, RAM and ROM, looking for interesting and amusing things. You could try just PEEKing at random addresses, simply to see the sort of thing you can find. Try #3FE7A PEEK, then #3FE8A PEEK, then #3FE9A, #3FEAA, #3FEBA and #3FECA. If you have a version 1BB HP-28C then these addresses contain the version number message and the HP copyright notice. A piece of software is protected by copyright law if it has a copyright notice included; even if the copyright notice is not available to be seen! If you have some other version of the HP-28 then the version and copyright information should be somewhere in the same part of ROM. You must get the nybble boundary right - in version 1BB you can try #3FE78, #3FE7A, #3FE7C, #3FE7E and so on, but if you try an odd number such as #3FE79 or #3FE7B then the nybbles will be paired off incorrectly and you will not see a meaningful message.

For another example try #FCCF PEEK. On a version 1BB HP-28C this will give the string "CONTINUE". That is the full name of the non-programmable operation CONT - once you have found a name like this you can PEEK at the numbers immediately following it; these might contain the addresses of some subprograms which check the stack and so on, and then you will find the address of the operation itself. To make it easier to read the contents of the address you have PEEKed as a set of addresses, replace "DUMMYSTR" in the PEEK program with #0. This means that X2 will be read as a binary number, so PEEK will now give the contents of the PEEKed address as a string of hexadecimal digits, which are easier to read but are stored in reverse order. Try replacing "DUMMYSTR" with #0, then PEEK at the address immediately after the name CONTINUE, address #FCDF. On a version 1BB you will see the binary integer #2F901058A05334. (Set wordsize 64 and HEX mode to see the whole binary integer.) This means that the sixteen nybbles of memory immediately after CONTINUE are 43350A850109F200 (the leading 0s are not seen because the display does not show leading zeros in binary integers). These are the addresses of three subprograms, themselves stored in reverse order: 05334, 1058A and 02F90. The first address is that of a subprogram which makes some introductory tests, the second address is that of the CONTINUE command itself - this is the address that I gave in the previous chapter, as though pulled out of thin air. Now you know how the address was discovered, and you can trying finding others the same way.

Well, you might want to try using PEEK at random for a while, but eventually you will realize that there is just too much ROM for it all to be examined at random. It is much better to write programs which use PEEK to search for some characteristic piece of information. Say you want to find where the clock value is stored. Since it changes, it must be stored in RAM, so you could write a program to examine every 16 nybble location from the top of ROM to the top of RAM (from #40000 to #4FFFF on an HP-28C). The program should PEEK at each location twice, and see if its contents have changed - if so then this is an address which keeps changing, and it could be the clock location. Of course other addresses might change too, and the clock might be stored in more than one 16 nybble register, so you would then have to examine more closely each register that did change.

Instead of using a binary integer in X2 to read the PEEKed address as a back-to-front binary number, we could use a program to decode a source text string into a result string of hexadecimal digits. This is not simple, here is a program to do it; see if you can write a shorter version.

```
<<  RCWS  9  STWS      ;save word size, reset it to 9 bits
    ""  ROT            ;put initially empty result string in level 2
    1  OVER  SIZE      ;set up limits to loop over bytes in source
                       string
    FOR  J            ;start the loop, with counter J
    DUP  J  DUP  SUB  ;pick byte (character) at position J
    NUM              ;convert it to a number
    256  +           ;add 256 to make it a 3-digit hexadecimal
                      number
    R->B  ->STR      ;turn it into a string of hexadecimal digits
```

```
    DUP  5  DUP  SUB  ;pick least significant hexadecimal digit
    SWAP  4  DUP  SUB ;pick next digit, string has 3 digits so can
                         get 0
    + ROT  SWAP  +    ;append digits, in reverse order, to result
                       string
    SWAP  NEXT        ;recover source string in level 1, end loop
    DROP              ;discard source string when loop finished
    SWAP  STWS  >>    ;replace original word size


  'DECOD'  STO        ;store as a decode program
```

Try #FCDF PEEK again with "DUMMYSTR" in X2, then press DECOD.
After a short while, you should see "43350A850109F200". This method
has the advantages that the result is the right way round and you do
not lose leading zeros.

If you use PEEK in a larger program then you can save a lot of time
by rewriting PEEK so it does not have to PURGE and recreate X1 and
X2 every time. It would be enough just to change the second binary
number in X1 so as to change the address being PEEKed. You could
also set the wordsize to 64, and avoid saving it and restoring it at
the beginning and end of each PEEK. Once you have gained some
confidence, you might try to rewrite PEEK to make it faster and
shorter, by reading the PEEK address directly off the stack (using
the address given by pointer D1), and by using pieces of code from
ROM to replace parts of the program. If you write a really good
PEEK of your own, submit it for publication in a club journal so
that other HP-28 users will take advantage of it, and will recognize
your brilliance!

4.6 And now a POKE command. Once you have examined the insides of
the operating system, you may well want to change some things; of
course you can only change the contents of RAM. The normal name in
BASIC for a command which does this is POKE. A simple way to write
a POKE program is to change PEEK; after all you just want to write
something to a selected address, instead of reading from that
address. The natural way to use POKE is to give a value to be

POKEd, then the address to POKE, and then to execute POKE. To make
POKE work like this, we can rewrite PEEK so it will store in X2 the
value to be POKEd, then create a list of binary numbers which
include the POKE address, then execute the list as a program, then
stop. This is just the reverse of what PEEK does. Here is the
layout of memory in an HP-28C which contains the machine code part
of such a program. Yet again, if you have a memory-expanded HP-28C,
an HP-28S, or some other new model, then check Appendix E.

address (hex)	contents (hex)	equivalent instruction	explanation
4FF5F	20		length in bytes of object name 'X1'
4FF61	8513		object name 'X1' nybbles inverted
4FF65	20		length in bytes of name, again
4FF67	69A20		address of list definition
4FF6C	07A20		address defining first binary integer
4FF71	51000		length of binary integer+5 in nybbles

--------------- First binary integer begins below ---------------------

address	contents	equivalent	explanation
4FF76	B7FF4	REL(5) 5	address of program start
4FF7B	133	AD1EX	exchange A with D1 to save pointer
4FF7E	103	R3=A	save A (old D1) in scratch R3
4FF81	6E00	GOTO (*)+E	jump forward over intervening info
4FF85	0		fill out to end of binary integer

--------------- First binary integer finishes here --------------------

address	contents	equivalent	explanation
4FF86	07A20		address defining 2nd binary integer
4FF8B	51000		length, +5 to allow for length count

--------------- Second binary integer begins below --------------------

address	contents	equivalent	explanation
4FF90	1F0FFF4	D1=4FFF0	set pointer D1 to address of X2
4FF97	15BF	A=DAT1l0	copy register pointed to by D1 into A
4FF9B	6E00	GOTO (*)+E	jump over intervening stuff again
4FF9F	B		fill out last nybble of binary integer

--------------- Second binary integer finishes here -------------------

4FFA0	07A20		address defining 3rd binary integer
4FFA5	51000		length +5

--------------- Third binary integer begins here ----------------------

4FFAA	1F00000	D1=00000	set pointer D1 to address to POKE
4FFB1	159F	DAT1=A 10	copy register A to this address
4FFB5	6E00	GOTO (*)+E	jump over intervening stuff again
4FFB9	0		filler

--------------- Third binary integer ends here -----------------------

4FFBA	07A20		address defining 4th binary integer
4FFBF	51000		length +5

--------------- Fourth binary integer begins here ---------------------

4FFC4	113	A=R3	recover pointer from R3
4FFC7	131	D1=A	put original pointer value in D1
4FFCA	142	A=DAT0 A	get address of next command address
4FFCD	164	D0=D0+ 5	add 5 to D0 to point to following command
4FFD0	808C	PC=(A)	jump to the address given by A

--------------- Fourth and last binary integer of list ends here ------

4FFD4	09F20		address defining end of composite object
4FFD9	A7000		length in nybbles of object, name
4FFDE	20		length in bytes of object name 'X2'
4FFE0	8523		object name, 'X2'
4FFE4	20		length of name, again
4FFE6	E4A20		address defining a text string
4FFEB	51000		length+5 in nybbles
4FFF0	16-nybble dummy string		string to be replaced by PEEK result
			extends to top of memory at 4FFFF

This POKE is similar to PEEK, except that X2 at #4FF90 now has the value to be POKEd, and #4FFAA contains the address to which this will be written.

```
< RCWS ROT ROT SWAP       ;get word size, put value to POKE in
                          ;level 1
   'X2' DUP PURGE          ;purge old copy of X2
   ROT 28 STWS SLB         ;shift POKE address one byte left
   64 STWS                 ;set full word size so nothing will be
                          ;lost
   #E6F95100000F1 +        ;add POKE address into program
   #E63013314FF7B SWAP     ;put first binary integer on top
   #E6FB514FFF0F1 SWAP     ;put 2nd binary integer next in stack
   #C808461241131311       ;third binary now in level 1, put in 4th
   4 ->LIST                ;convert to a list of 4 binary integers
   'X1' DUP PURGE STO      ;purge X1 and store list in it
   STO STWS                ;store POKE value in X2, replace old
                          ;word size
   #4FF76 SYSEVAL >>       ;use SYSEVAL to execute POKE, then stop

'POKE' STO                ;store the POKE program
```

Once more, check Appendix E if your HP-28 is not a standard HP-28C.
The program could be written in other ways, but writing it by
modifying PEEK shows how it is often possible to modify a piece of
code to do a new job. (You can create POKE by doing 'PEEK RCL
EDIT and storing the new program.) In a similar way it is possible
to use pieces of code from ROM to do a job for you, instead of
writing a completely new program.

To use POKE, put the value to poke, as a text string encoded by COD,
on level 2, put the address to POKE this into on level 1 of the
stack, then do POKE. POKE only modifies RAM, if the address you
give is not the address of a piece of RAM, then the program will
run, but nothing will be changed. POKE is dangerous - you can hang
up the HP-28, or stop the display working, or get a Memory Lost if
you are not careful, so do not use it at random. If you prefer not
to use COD, you can express the value that you want to POKE as a
binary integer, (a binary integer takes exactly the same amount of
memory as an 8-byte text string), but remember to write all the
digits of the binary integer in reverse order, and to allow for

leading zeros in the binary integer. Thus to POKE a hex string 0123456789ABCDEF, use #FEDCBA9876543210. This version of POKE pokes sixteen nybbles, again after some practice you might like to try writing your own version. Good luck!

One suitable use for POKE is to set the correct time in the system clock, so there is no need for a separate correction factor. The system clock is stored in two parts of RAM. 8 nybbles beginning at address #407F8 hold a 32 bit number which is decremented (reduced by 1) 8192 times a second. The counter is decremented by a clock circuit, not the CPU which is doing its own work. Each time this counter goes through zero, it sets an "interrupt request" flag. The CPU checks this from time to time and if it is set then the CPU stops what it is doing, checks what caused the interrupt, and resets the counter to count for another minute without interrupting; in other words the CPU adds 8192*60 to the counter. Then the CPU adds 8192*60 to a separate 48 bit counter which is stored in the 12 nybbles beginning at #4F003. This value is the time at which the clock will be updated next. (If you POKE a big number into #407F8 then it will be a long time before the clock is updated, so your HP-28 will not turn off after 10 minutes.)

When you read the system clock with #123E, the 48 bit counter is read, then the value in the 32 bit counter is read and subtracted from it. This should be the time now, and by POKEing the correct value into the 48 bit counter you can make it so. A 48 bit counter updated by 8192 every second will count for nearly 1089 years before it goes back to zero, so you could use the clock as a calendar too, but not to count all the way from 1 AD. Nor should you set the time so near to its top value that it will cycle back to zero and change the time while you are still using the HP-28 and not some even newer HP toy. If you want to use the clock as a calendar too then it might be reasonable to set it to zero at the beginning of January 1901. The HP-28C does not have room for a full set of calendar functions so it is best not to use its clock as a calendar but simply set it to zero at the beginning of the present day. That will minimize the effects of inaccuracies in the clock, and so I suggest doing the same on an HP-28S.

Let us then use POKE to correct the clock, without bothering to use it as a calendar. In point 3.2 we obtained a correction for the clock and stored it in the variable called KOR. If you no longer have that variable, or if your clock is no longer accurate, then set KOR to zero, and then recalculate it as described in point 3.2. Then recall KOR to the stack, multiply it by 3600 to convert it to seconds, and again by 8192 to turn it to counts. This is the correction we are going to add to the system clock. Now PEEK the clock value, it is simplest to treat it as a binary number, so VISIT the PEEK program and replace the string "DUMMYSTR" with the binary number #0, if you have not already done so. Type #4F003 PEEK to get the 48 bit part of the clock, then press + to add the correction. Now type #4F003 POKE to put back the 48 bit clock, corrected to give the right time. VISIT the TIME program and remove the steps KOR + which should no longer be needed, and PURGE KOR. Press TIME to see if the clock is now correct. The clock might be one minute slow, see below, or if something has gone wrong then it might be completely wrong; in that case calculate a correction again as described in point 3.2, then repeat the instructions above. As ever, check Appendix E if yours is not a version 1BB HP-28C.

The 48 bit clock at #4F003 might have been updated by a minute between the time when you PEEKed at #4F003 and the time you POKEd the corrected value. If so, then the corrected time will be a minute slow, and you will need to add another minute to the correction - so PEEK at #4F003 again, add 60*8192 to the result, and POKE it back to #4F003 again. If you are unlucky then the clock might update itself again just when you do this, so check TIME, and if necessary repeat the correction. Once the TIME is right, you might want to change PEEK again to use a text string instead of a binary number.

4.7 Jumping to Conclusions. Writing HP-28 machine language programs takes a lot of memory. Much of this is used for the ancillary programs such as PEEK or COD, not for the machine language programs themselves. Even so, it is better to use SYSEVAL to execute pieces of programs from ROM, rather than write your own machine language programs which take up valuable space in RAM. If you have an HP-28 with more than 2K of user memory in it, then you will be able to store more programs, but after a Memory Lost you will have more work putting the programs in again. In some cases, such as very short programs, or programs which need to be independent of the HP-28 version, it is still better to use your own machine language programs. The interrupt off program and PEEK are examples of this. In addition there are operations which can only be carried out by machine language programs.

In general though, it is best to look for pieces of programs in ROM to provide new commands that you need. If you want a programmable version of a non-programmable operation then write a program to look for the name of that operation in ROM by using PEEK. If you can find the name then check the instructions that come after the name; they usually consist of a set of addresses, one of which should carry out the required operation. Then you can use this address and SYSEVAL to include the command in programs. The addresses ahead of this one usually check that the HP-28 is in the required state, and that the stack contains any objects needed by the operation. It is important to make sure you check the same things in your own program! In the same way, if you want a command which is similar to a programmable command then it is best to use PEEK to examine the addresses which make up that command. Say you want to write a command similar to PIXEL; PEEK lets you find that PIXEL begins at address 1BE87 (in version 1BB HP-28Cs), so try PEEKing at this address and the ones after to find the addresses of the subprograms used to execute PIXEL.

Once you have found the addresses which make up a command, you can use SYSEVAL to execute the subprograms which make up that command, one by one. Unfortunately, SYSEVAL cannot execute a whole string of

bprograms; you cannot get it to execute part of a program. If you
) #XXXXX SYSEVAL then SYSEVAL reads the 5 nybbles at address
XXXX, jumps to the address given by those five nybbles, and carries
it the machine language instructions beginning at that address.
ne of two things can happen, as shown below:

ase 1:

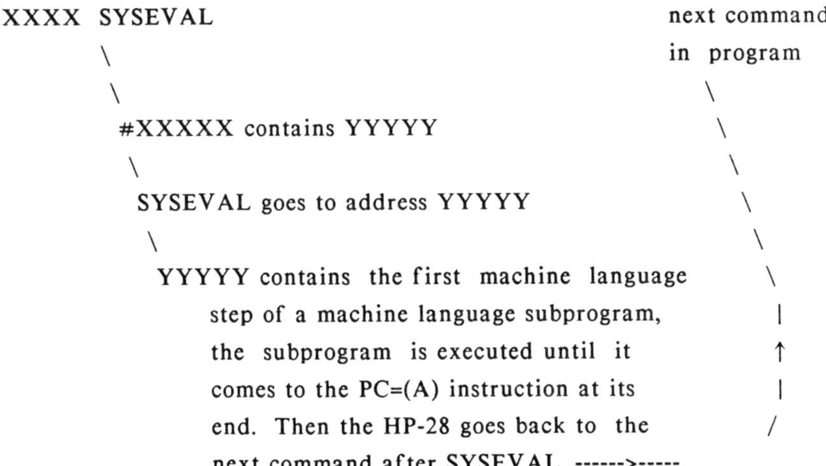

i this case, the HP-28 carries out one machine language subprogram,
ien goes back to the command after SYSEVAL.

ase 2:

In this special case the address 02C67 contains

the first machine language step of a machine language subprogram, which creates a new program thread. Once the new thread is established the HP-28 carries on executing subprograms whose addresses come after 02C67 in the thread, until the subprogram 02F90 is reached. When this is executed, it kills the thread and returns the HP-28 to the previous thread, which was the one containing SYSEVAL.

In other words, SYSEVAL can:

EITHER execute one machine language subprogram whose starting address is stored at XXXXX

OR it can execute a whole RPL subprogram whose starting address is stored at XXXXX and which program begins with 02C67, is made up of other subprograms, and ends with 029F0.

However SYSEVAL cannot execute part of an RPL subprogram; it can NOT do the following:

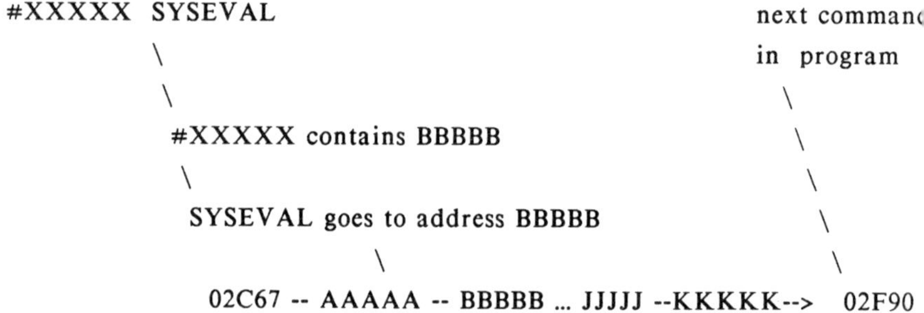

In this case we would like SYSEVAL to execute PART of an RPL subprogram, but SYSEVAL is not designed to do that.

What SYSEVAL does is start at the beginning of a machine code subprogram, execute it all, and finish at the end, or start at the beginning of an RPL subprogram, (marked by 02C67) execute each subprogram within that RPL subprogram, and finish at the end. SYSEVAL goes from commencement to conclusion, it cannot jump to the middle of an RPL subprogram or of a machine language subprogram and carry on to the conclusion.

The point of this section, and of its title, is that it is often useful to jump into the middle of a machine language subprogram or an RPL subprogram and execute that program to its conclusion. As SYSEVAL cannot do this we need our own machine language programs to do these things. Of course there may be times when you want to execute a piece from a subprogram, without coming to its end. That is more difficult; in general you have to put that piece of program in RAM and execute it there, unless you can work out some way to exit from a subprogram in the middle - this might be possible if a test in the subprogram allows the subprogram to terminate early.

Jumping into the middle of a machine language subprogram is not too bad. You need to find the address you want to go, then execute the single machine code instruction GOVLNG (GO Very LoNG) that allows a machine language program to jump to any other place in memory. Presumably the address to go to will be in level 1 of the stack, as is the case with SYSEVAL, so our machine language subprogram must take the address from the stack and drop the stack one level. Once our subprogram has jumped to the machine level subprogram in ROM, that subprogram will execute to the end, then it will use PC=(A) to go directly to the command following our machine language subprogram, so our subprogram does not itself need to finish with PC=(A). The machine language part of this subprogram would look like this:

address (hex)	contents (hex)	equivalent instruction		explanation
4FFF4	4FFF9	REL(5)	5	address where machine code begins
4FFF9	8DXXXXX	GOVLNG	XXXXX	go to address XXXXX (XXXXX must be stored back to front)

This is less than 16 nybbles long, so we can write a program which works the same way as PEEK and POKE, but stores all the machine code in one binary integer at the top of memory.

```
<<  RCWS  SWAP  52  STWS   ;save the present word size and set it to
    SLB  SLB  SLB  SLB      ;52 shift the address 32 bits to the left
    # D84FFF90  +          ;add the address to the beginning of the
                           ;program (the 0 makes it an exact number
                           ;of bytes long)
    'X2'  DUP  PURGE  STO  ;store the program in X2 at the top of
    STWS                   ;memory, put back the previous word size
    # 4FFF4  SYSEVAL  >>   ;jump into the machine code

'JMPM  STO                 ;store the program "JuMP to Machine
                           ;code"
```

This program stores the machine language code while the binary word size is set to 52 bits, so the word is stored in a field whose length is rounded up to the next multiple of 4 bits, which is 52 bits anyway. That means the GOVLNG instruction is stored at address 4FFF9, so SYSEVAL has to jump to address 4FFF9, and this address is given at 4FFF4. As an example of using JMPM, try putting an object on the stack, then doing #205F JMPM. This jumps directly into the machine language part of the DUP command, so the object on the stack will be duplicated. It is clearly quicker to use DUP itself, but the point of JMPM is that it lets you experiment by jumping to any part of the machine language in ROM. Jumping into ROM can easily lead to Memory Lost, so it is as well that this program is short and does not use any other subprograms - you can re-enter it after a Memory Lost and carry on testing. If you want to use a piece of machine language code in ROM which finishes with a RTN instruction then rewrite JMPM so it executes GOSBVL (8F instead of 8D) and is followed by A=DAT0 A, D0=D0+5, PC=(A).

Jumping into the middle of an RPL subprogram is more challenging. I shall use this as an example to explain details of three extra machine code techniques for the HP-28:

1. We must reset the thread pointer (in D0) so that it points to the thread containing the target address.

2. We shall read the address directly out of the stack (using D1), and drop the stack, using machine code.

3. Instead of storing the machine language code at the top of memory, we shall use a special system object which is recognized as a string of machine language code to be executed immediately. This can be stored in the middle of a program anywhere, and although it is displayed only as "System Object" when you look at a program, it is executed correctly. A piece of machine code stored like this in the middle of a program in a higher level language is called in-line machine code.

The RPL part of the program to do all this will be:

```
<<  RR  RL                 ;check for a binary integer in level 1
    "ABCDEFGHIJKLMNO" ;string to be replaced by machine code,
    "B"  >>                ;see below used only to check the program


'JMPR  STO                 ;store the program "JuMP to RPL code"
```

The instructions RR RL check there is at least one object on the stack and that it is a binary integer, but do not change it. If level 1 does not contain a binary integer then the program will stop and display an error message here. The following string will be replaced by in-line machine code which will transfer the program pointer from this program to the RPL subprogram into which we want to jump. If this jump is successful then at the end of that RPL subprogram, we shall jump directly back to the program which used JMPR; this means we shall not go back into JMPR, so the "B" will not be put on the stack. If you use this program and "B" is put on the stack then there is something wrong with your version of JMPR.

The machine code program to do all this is as follows:

address (hex)	content (hex)	equivalent instruction	explanation
?????	69C20	MCODE	address defining a string of machine code
?????	32000	LEN	length of string, stored back to front
?????	147	C=DAT1 A	get address of level 1 object
?????	174	D1=D1+ 5	add 5 to D1, then add 1 to D, this in effect
?????	E7	D=D+1 A	drops the item in level 1
?????	137	CD1EX	put old level 1 item address in D1
?????	179	D1=D1+ A	add 10 to D1, so it points to the binary value
?????	143	A=DAT1 A	copy first 5 nibs from old level 1 object to A
?????	130	D0=A	put this address in D0
?????	164	D0=D0+5	next address will be 5 nibs forward
?????	135	D1=C	restore stack pointer from C to D1
?????	808C	PC=(A)	jump to address now given by A

The addresses are all given as ????? because these instructions will be carried out as in-line code, which is position independent. The first two instructions are not really machine code. The first is the address of a subprogram which tells the HP-28 to treat the following as a string of machine code instructions. The second is five nybbles giving the length of the string, including these five nybbles themselves. Both of these first two are stored back to front; they tell the HP-28 that this object is a string, not of text, but of machine code instructions, so the address of the next subprogram to be executed does not come immediately after the 69C20, instead it is LEN nybbles further along. This means D0 will be incremented by LEN nybbles before A=DAT0 A and PC=(A) are used to jump to the next subprogram. Normally this would mean that the next instruction to be carried out would be "B" in JMPR. In this case, the purpose of the machine code is to change the pointer D0, so "B" will only be put on the stack if the machine code program did not change the pointer.

The next instruction reads the value pointed to by D1. D1 points to a place which contains the address of the level 1 object. The stack itself is just a list of addresses, each of which points to the place where the corresponding stack object is actually stored. The objects themselves are stored elsewhere, they might be variables, stored at the top of RAM, or they might be objects which exist only in the stack, stored in a separate part of RAM, or they might be commands which are in ROM. The list of addresses usually has room for extra addresses so that the stack can be expanded; if the level 1 object is dropped, then D1 moves up by 5 nybbles, to point at the previous address, and the number of free places in the stack increases by 1. The number of free places is stored in the A field of CPU register D; if this number ever becomes zero then the list must be expanded, so more memory needs to be made free. (The process of "garbage collection" is used to do this; it looks for pieces of memory which have been used but are now free and moves things around so that the stack list can be extended. If this is not possible then the message "Insufficient Memory" is shown.)   A schematic diagram of all this is shown below.   The next two instructions D1=D1+ 5 and D=D+1 A are used to drop an object from the stack; the stack "forgets" about this object, although it is still stored in memory and can be read.   If the object existed only in the stack then it becomes a candidate for deletion the next time garbage collection is carried out.

.

.

.

```
                 address of level 3 object
                 address of level 2 object
D1---> address of level 1 object---  D =    n, number of places
         (room for another address)   |      left in stack
         (room for another address)   |      address list  before  and
                        .              |       it  runs  out of space
                        .              |      "garbage collection" is
                        .              |      needed to provide more room
     (room for nth extra address)      |
                                       |
                                    level  1
                                    object
```

Schematic of stack control by D1, the stack address list, and D

Although the program has "dropped" the object from level 1, the address of that object is still stored in register C. That object is the binary integer telling JMPR what address to jump to, so we now need to read that address and jump to it. The next instruction, CD1EX brings the object's address to D1, and at the same time saves the previous contents of D1 in register C. At this point, D1 points to the beginning of the binary integer, the actual value begins 10 nybbles further, past the address of the object definition and the object length. The next program step adds A (decimal 10) to D1 so as to point at the value itself. A=DAT1 A   reads this value into register A.   At this point the program is ready to jump to the address given to JMPR, but D0 is still pointing to the next instruction in JMPR ("B"). D0=A is used to copy the same address to the program pointer and D0=D0+ 5 is used to point D0 to the next RPL instruction past the present one. These two steps make sure that the RPL instruction at the address given to JMPR, and the instructions after it, will be carried out, unlike SYSEVAL which carries out just one instruction. D1=C restores the original value of D1, and finally PC=(A) jumps from the thread of the JMPR program into the thread beginning at the address given to JMPR.

If you find this beyond comprehension, try reading it again and drawing some simple diagrams, like the schematic shown above. You might also find it helpful to read the Assembler chapter of the HP-71B FORTH/Assembler ROM manual, particularly the section on FORTH primitives. Look in Appendix D for more details too. If you still do not understand, follow the example below, the results will be interesting even if you do not understand them!

To enter the program, type in and store JMPR as shown above. Make sure you have the PEEK and POKE programs in your HP-28 too. You will need a CODE program as well. If you do not have enough room in memory for all these programs then you may need to delete some programs. If you still have too little room for the CODE program then use the following short version:

<< B->R CHR >> 'CDE STO

This can be used to build up a string of binary bytes, given the individual bytes that make it up. For example to create the binary bytes

1A3C5F

```
do: HEX              ;set HEX mode
    #A1 CDE          ;create the character equivalent to byte 1A
    #C3 CDE +        ;create byte 3C and append it to 1A
    #F5 CDE +        ;create byte 5F and add it to the string
```

To set up the JMPR program do the following (take care to avoid mistakes):

1. Put the programs PEEK, POKE, JMPR (as shown above) and CODE (or CDE as above) in the HP-28. Make sure JMPR is the first variable - if need be do { JMPR } ORDER to put JMPR first.

2. Use PEEK to find the beginning of the text string which is to be replaced. We need to change the definition from that of a text string to that of an in-line program string, so we need the five

bytes ahead of the text string too. You should find this at address #4FF1C which PEEKs the string "N*0░ABC". If you DECODe this you will see E4A2032000142434. 02A4E is the address of the subprogram which defines a text string, we need to replace this with 02C96. If you have the CODE program then you can edit the original text string to change this and then use CODE to turn the text string back into eight bytes to be POKEd. If you do not have CODE then use CDE instead. Do 3 8 SUB to get the piece which is not to be changed, then do #96 CDE #2C CDE + SWAP + to set up the new string. In either case, use #4FF1C POKE to put the new object definition into JMPR.

3. Now we use PEEK to get the text string itself and change it. We need to create a 15 byte long machine language program to replace the text string "ABCDEFGHIJKLMNO", but PEEK and POKE both work on eight byte strings, so we need to do the job in two parts. We can deal with seven bytes, leaving one unchanged, and then with the other eight bytes. First PEEK address #4FF24 which should show up as "░ABCDEFG". The first byte is 00, part of the string length definition which we do not want to change, the other seven bytes are to be replaced by 147174E7137179. Use DECOD to decode the string and edit it to replace all except the first four digits, then use CODE to set up the new string. If you do not have CODE then do 1 2 SUB to keep the first two bytes, then #17 CDE + #47 CDE + #7E CDE + #31 CDE + #17 CDE + #97 CDE + to build up the rest of the string. (You could use binary integers to build up the strings instead of using CODE or CDE.) Note that the first byte is "A" which does not need to be replaced. Use POKE to put the new string at address #4FF24.

4. The remaining eight bytes to be replaced are at address #4FF34. There is no need to PEEK there, unless you want to check that everything is still working and that address still contains "HIJKLMNO". This is to be replaced by the rest of the machine code: 143130164135808C. As this is all a single string of hexadecimal digits it is probably fastest to do:

HEX 64 STWS #C808531461031341 #4FF34 POKE

5. To check this has worked, do 'JMPR' VISIT and you should see:
<< RR RL System Object "B" >>
The text string has been replaced by an in-line string of machine code which the HP-28 cannot decompile, so the code is displayed only as a System Object. Although the decompiler cannot display the in-line code, it does recognize the code to the extent that the "B" after it is displayed correctly. You can VISIT or RCL this program, but if you try to edit it then the in-line code will be replaced by the two words 'System' and 'Object', as was explained earlier.

6. If you have made any mistakes then trying to VISIT JMPR will probably hang up the HP-28 (stop it working). Try doing a System Halt - this might bring the HP-28 back to normal, but most likely you will get a Memory Lost, and will have to start over again. This is the sort of occasion that makes one wish the HP-28 provided some way of reading programs back in instead of requiring you to type them in again from the keyboard.

JMPR is provided here as an example of in-line code, and as an experimental tool. For example the NEXT operation is not programmable, but in point 3.11 we saw that instructions beginning at #E514 provide the instructions used to do the NEXT operation. If you use PEEK to decipher NEXT you will find that it is a long string of subprogram addresses, beginning with 07A4A which is stored at address E530. You can use JMPR to jump into different parts of the NEXT program and see what they do. The first few are:

#E530 JMPR -clears the display
#E535 JMPR -clears the display
#E53A JMPR -clears the display after a short wait
#E53F JMPR -brings a binary integer to the stack
etc.
#E55D JMPR -drops two objects from the stack, then initiates NEXT

You can write a program to execute just part of NEXT by using this:

```
<<  1  1                 ;put two numbers on stack to be dropped
    #E55D  JMPR          ;jump to the main part of NEXT
    #C148  SYSEVAL       ;hide the menu labels
    #A28B  SYSEVAL       ;show the menu labels, this shows the current
>>                       ;menu activated by jumping into the code.
                         ;End the program
```

Try using this - you will find it does not behave exactly like NEXT, you may be able to make use of the differences.

4.8 POKEing the key buffer. This chapter has already described how to put non-programmable commands into programs, but looking for the SYSEVAL values can take a long time. Another way of making a program carry out a non-programmable command is to make it seem that the appropriate key has been pressed by POKEing the keystroke into the key buffer. The key buffer is in the 16 bytes from address #4F03A to #4F058, with keystroke 1 at address #4F03A, keystroke 2 at #4F03C, and on up to keystroke 0 at #4F058. The number of the most recently executed keystroke is stored as one nybble at address #4F038, and the number of the most recently stored keystroke is in the nybble at #4F039. Each HP-28 key has its own keycode, as shown in the figure below - my thanks to Kim Holm for providing it. To pretend that the "lower case" key has been pressed, for example, a program can POKE the binary integer #0A10 into address #4F038. When the program stops running the HP-28 reads this string from the key buffer, assumes the last keystroke read was at position 0 in the key buffer, there is one more keystroke to deal with at position 1, and the key is key 0A - so it sets lower case mode. Here's something to amaze your friends; write a program which does: << #5149442E8050 #4F038 POKE >>, store it in a variable KK, then press the KK key. The keycodes are for SHIFT, CATALOG, F, USE, NEXT, and you will see all of this carried out! Actually, you do not need to store a separate keystroke for the SHIFT key, you can just add #80 to the key to be shifted, for example you can POKE #BF10 into the key buffer to carry out PREV. Two warnings - the key buffer is only read when your program stops, and 7F or FF (ATTN) makes the HP-28 stop reading the buffer and restart your program.

```
[41]  [42]  [48]  [47]  [46]  [44]
[35]  [36]  [3C]  [3B]  [3A]  [38]
[29]  [2A]  [30]  [2F]  [2E]  [2C]
[1D]  [1E]  [24]  [23]  [22]  [20]
[11]  [12]  [18]  [17]  [16]  [14]
[   06   ]  [0C]  [08]  [0A]  [08]
```

```
[51]  [4F]  [4C]  [49]  [4A]  [4B]
[80]  [43]  [40]  [3D]  [3E]  [3F]
[   37   ]  [34]  [31]  [32]  [33]
[2D]  [2B]  [28]  [25]  [26]
[21]  [1F]  [1C]  [19]  [1A]
[15]  [13]  [10]  [0D]  [0E]
[7F]  [07]  [04]  [01]  [02]
```

4.9 Where next? This chapter has provided some neat "customization" tricks and a set of programs to be used by explorers, particularly those who already know something about Saturn machine code and want to try it out on the HP-28. If you want to learn more or share your discoveries, join a user club! A list is in Appendix A, some club journals have already published machine language programs. If enough interest is shown then maybe someone will even write a book specifically about HP-28 machine code programming.

CHAPTER 5 - FURTHER CUSTOMIZATION

This chapter describes some additional sorts of customization; such as hardware modifications, especially adding extra memory to the HP-28C and speeding it up, and customization of the USER menu, particularly using HP-28S subdirectories. As not everyone will be willing to pull their nice new (and expensive) HP-28 to bits, I shall begin the first part with a change requiring no alterations at all.

5.1 A few extra labels. The label above the left hand keyboard provides useful information, but not nearly enough - it gives no TYPE numbers, and a list of the flags that control features of the HP-28 would be very useful too. Both sorts of information can easily be written on an adhesive label which can be stuck to the HP-28. Other information worth recording is the amount of memory used by different objects, or the numbers used to get different menus with the HP-28S MENU command or the HP-28C MENU program described in point 3.11. As mentioned in that point, the MENU command is most helpful when you want to hold the HP-28 in one hand, with the left hand keyboard folded under. This means that the menu numbers should be written on a label stuck above the display. The same label could have a list of flag numbers and descriptions on it too, so that you would not have to turn the HP-28 over or look for a manual when using MENU or flags. The label could also describe any special use you may make of some of the flags 1 to 30; it could even have some SYSEVAL values if you use them.

Further information worth having includes the default limits of the plot area, and the formulae for display positions, given in the PLOT section of the Reference Manual. You might like to have a list of the different looping commands - do you always remember that FOR requires a name but START does not? Again, you may want to remind yourself which objects and structures are automatically completed for you by the HP-28 and which ones you have to complete yourself. I often forget that, whereas END is automatically put at the end of a program if needed, STEP or NEXT are not. You can doubtless think of other things to put on such labels. The point is that you can customize your HP-28 by making your own labels and sticking them above the display, and over the label above the left keyboard. If you wish, you can put labels on the back instead of, or as well as, putting them inside. Labels on the back are more likely to get dirty or be torn off, but some companies (EduCALC for one, see Appendix A) sell soft leather cases which will keep an HP-18, an HP-19 or an HP-28 clean and protect labels stuck to it. A nice fold-away label was published in V1N4 of HPX Exchange, see Appendix A. One final point, if several people near you use HP-28s then it is worth having a label with your name on it attached to your HP-28 too.

* * *

The next part of this chapter describes the hardware inside the HP-28, and how you can modify it, concentrating on the HP-28C. This is not something to be done by the faint-hearted or the non-expert. I suggest you read through it all and only then decide whether to open up your HP-28: several organizations offer a service of putting extra memory into an HP-28C for you. Much of the information and pictures here come from studying an HP-28C bought for the HPCC club R&D project, this is just one of the advantages of belonging to a user club - you can share out the costs of an expensive project, and share in the discoveries that come from it. Even if you have no intention of opening up your HP-28 you may find this part interesting as it describes how the HP-28 works.

5.2 The memory problem. Most new HP-28C users take less than a day to decide they would like more memory in their HP-28C. The 1683 bytes of user memory (RAM) available after a reset can hold just over 100 real numbers or 300 program steps (or intermediate combinations of the two) but in practice there is room for less than that, since you need to store other things too. Some tricks that let you use less memory have been described in previous chapters, but eventually the question arises - can we put in more RAM? One of the things this chapter will show is how that can be done.

But first, why is so little RAM (Random Access Memory) available to users? There is 128K of ROM (Read Only Memory) where the built-in instructions are stored, yet only 2K bytes of RAM, with only about 1700 bytes available to the user. The HP-71B is controlled by a CPU chip similar to that in the HP-28, has 16K bytes RAM built in, and 4K RAM modules from HP can be added to the HP-71B, so why is there not the equivalent of at least one 4K module in the HP-28C? Well, the Saturn CPU chip in the HP-71B and the HP-28C (and 18C) sends and receives data only 4 bits (half a byte, or one nybble) at a time, so as to reduce the number of data lines that have to be fitted on the circuit boards. To speed up operations each RAM and ROM chip has a "controller" which stores the address currently being read or written - that way the Saturn CPU does not have to send out a complete address every time it requests or sends some data. Instead, the address is updated by each chip after each read or write; at the next read or write the chip checks whether the current address is on board that chip, and responds if necessary. This means the RAM used with an HP-28 cannot be just any old RAM chip bought off the shelf; it has to come with a controller. HP make their own RAM chips for the Saturn with 1K bytes and a controller built in. A single 4K memory module for the HP-71B contains four such 1LG8 chips; to put 4K of RAM into the HP-28C, HP would have had to design it so that four such chips could be built in. These chips are normally mounted inside larger units called hybrids, but there is only a small amount of space inside each hybrid, and there is very little room for hybrids on the HP-28 circuit board. As HP also build small amounts of RAM memory into the display driver hybrid chips, that is where they put the RAM of the HP-28C, thus reducing the number of chips on the circuit board.

Apart from the size limits, a further design restriction was that the HP-28 had to pass tests on its ability to withstand various trials, including a 1 meter drop, and the only way they could have built more RAM into the HP-28C while sticking to these strict tests would have been to use a new type of RAM chip or display hybrid. As we know, they did this later, on the HP-19B and the HP-28S, but the first calculator of this type, the HP-18C, was designed to use only

2K of RAM. The HP-28C software was written later and allowed extra RAM chips to be added. (For example there is the message complaining that you are trying to edit a line which has more than 4096 characters; the HP-28C can store a maximum of about 1600 characters, so this message is clearly a leftover from a design allowing for more RAM.) In the end though, the HP-28C was built using the same circuit board and RAM chips as the HP-18C, giving just 2K RAM; a year later more compact chips were used to produce the HP-28S with more memory. Still, as stated above, the HP-28C software, and its circuit design too, do allow HP-28C owners to add more RAM themselves; if you don't mind your HP-28C being more delicate than HP specifications allow, then you can build in more memory.

5.3 Memory configuration. To exchange information with memory, the Saturn CPU needs to know the address of that memory. A RAM or ROM chip can either always have the same address, or it can let the Saturn CPU choose an address for it. In the first case, the chip is said to be "hard addressed" - for example the instructions which control the fundamental operations of the HP-71B or the HP-28 need to be in a hard-addressed ROM. In the second case, the chip is "soft addressed", and the CPU must give it an address - selecting this address and telling it to the chip controller is called "configuration" - the CPU can do it either after a reset or every time the calculator/computer is turned on. The HP-71B needs to be able to configure itself when it turns on, since modules may have been plugged in or removed while it was off. Thus HP-71B plug-in RAM modules are soft addressed, and the internal 4K modules which are nearly identical are soft addressed too. A device such as the HP-18C which has a predetermined amount of ROM and RAM can have all its chip addresses chosen when the device is designed, so everything can be hard-addressed, and there is no need for a configuration process to be carried out. Fortunately for us, the HP-28C was built to perform a configuration process (maybe the designers planned to build the HP-28 so that extra modules could be plugged in) and does have signal lines which transmit the configuration commands. This means we can build HP-71B RAM modules into an HP-28C, and everything will work!

The simplest way to get some RAM that will respond to HP-28 configuration commands is to buy a 4K, 32K (or even 64K) plug-in memory module for the HP-71B, open it up, remove the RAM hybrid with its carrier board, and build that into the HP-28C. Some people have removed built-in 4K RAMs from their HP-71Bs, and replaced them with 32K RAMs - the 4K RAMs taken out of an HP-71B during such an operation are nearly the same as the 4K inside a plug-in module, and can be used as well. 4K modules can be bought from HP dealers, or from larger discount stores such as EduCALC, and that is where you can buy the 32K or 64K front-port HP-71B modules made by CMT. Zengrange in the UK also sell 32K RAM modules. If you do decide to add 32K to an HP-28C, be sure to buy it in the form of a front-loading HP-71B module, as the ones which go in the card reader port are larger (and more expensive). You may be able to buy a 32K RAM board without the module case, this is cheaper but of course the board is less well protected during transit. It may not be necessary to add 32K (or 64K) RAM - clearly some people may need this much, but remember there is no way to store all that information outside an HP-28C and then read it back in. Many people will find an extra 4K sufficient, and much cheaper!

* * *

WARNING! Opening up an HP-28 is not safe (for the HP-28) unless you have a suitable workplace and suitable tools. Otherwise just read this section and look at the pictures. If you do decide to open up your HP-28, it would still be wise to read the whole section first, and obtain all the necessary tools and components. It is no good opening up an HP-28C so as to put in some extra RAM if you do not yet have that RAM! In any case remember that opening up an HP-28C or HP-28S renders any warranty totally null and void!

If you really do want more memory than the HP-28C has, you might find a friend who needs less RAM and is willing to buy your HP-28C at a reduced price, then you can use that money towards the cost of an HP-28S. That is likely to be much cheaper and safer than adding extra memory to an HP-28C. On the other hand, you might want to have 64K, which is only possible on an HP-28C, or you might have other reasons for opening your HP-28C or HP-28S.

5.4 Opening it up. The HP-28 is not designed to be opened and repaired, so you have to cut it open or break into it. The chip to which you solder the additional RAM is exactly 1 cm. square: if you look at the back of the HP-28C then this chip's left-hand edge lies exactly along the right-hand edge of the upper left-hand rubber foot. If you have the right tools, you can study the photographs in this book and then cut a hole in the back to get at the chip, but the bender (the metal circle that makes the BEEP) is glued to the case near it so this requires great care.

To open the HP-28 from the front first take out the batteries and remove the stick-down overlays above the display and over the keyboard. If you do this carefully then you will be able to put the overlays back on cleanly later and the HP-28 will look as if nothing has been done to it. Try lifting up a corner of the overlay, then pushing a flat plastic card slowly under it and working it along the overlay, lifting it up slowly. A thin credit card or a British Telecom phonecard should do. (Our French friends should not use their telephone credit cards which are much thicker.) Below the overlays you will find a lot of round holes, with a small button in the middle of each one - see photograph 1. The little button in each hole is actually the top of a peg which comes up from the back of the case, goes through the hole, and spreads out to hold down the front of the case. You will have to remove the top of every peg by drilling down into it using a drill bit with a diameter slightly smaller than that of the hole. The figure below shows the peg and the drill from the side. You should drill down only just far enough to remove the top of the peg, so that it no longer prevents the front being separated from the back. If you manage to leave a little of the peg still standing in the hole then you will be able to put the HP-28 together more easily. NEVER, NEVER drill too far down, or you will drill into the keyboard contacts and ruin your HP-28.

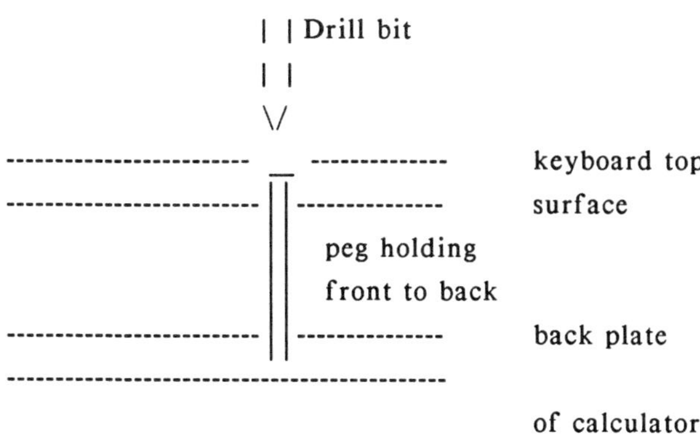

Drilling down to remove peg tops

Once you have drilled through all the pegs, remove the peg tops and the dirt left behind. Put some sticky tape over the whole keyboard so that the keys are held in place and will not fall out when you remove the keyboard from the case. Now pull the case apart. You may have to take care at the top left corner where the glue around the infra-red bulb holds the top and bottom together, but it can be worked free. Photograph 2 shows the circuit; the mat below the keys has been removed in this photograph to show the keyboard sandwich. The metal circle above the keyboard is the bender.

5.5 What's inside? You can now clearly see the circuit board. It carries CMOS circuits which are very susceptible to damage by static electricity, so take great care to avoid static - do not stand on a nylon carpet.   The large space above the circuit board is the battery compartment; the two springs which hold the batteries can be seen. These springs are held through two square holes seen above the display in photograph 1. The two springs standing up from the circuit board connect to the bender which is attached to the backplane.

Photograph 3 is an enlargement of the rear of the HP-28C circuit board. The board has been detached from the display to which it is normally held firmly. There is no need for you to separate the them together again properly. The two large chips are the two system ROMs. The other side has more circuitry with three chips - two large ones at left and right which are the display drivers, and a smaller CPU chip between them. All three are surface mounted and covered in epoxy to hold them down firmly. The HP-28S circuit is different, one chip carries the CPU, the ROM, and one display driver. A second chip is an industry standard 32K RAM chip, and the remaining chip carries all the other circuitry. The use of fewer chips means that the HP-28S layout is less complicated and therefore cheaper, so the HP-28S can have more RAM and yet can be sold at the same price as the HP-28C.

The display consists of 137 vertical columns by 32 horizontal lines, plus 7 annunciators (treated as vertical columns) and 1 horizontal line to control the annunciators. Each display dot or annunciator can thus be turned on if both its horizontal and vertical signals are powered up simultaneously for a moment. The left-hand display driver (looking from the front of the HP-28) controls the leftmost 77 vertical columns of the display, and the 7 individual display annunciators. The right-hand display driver controls the rightmost 60 vertical columns, and all 32 horizontal lines. If you have ever played with SYSEVAL, you have probably found some addresses which turn on all of the left-hand half of the display, and a small part of the right-hand half as well, but not the annunciators. This is because these addresses carry out some operation which turns on ALL of the left hand display driver, but leave the right-hand display driver unchanged.

We can be sure that the middle chip on the other side is the CPU because it connects directly to the two springs which drive the bender. The HP-71B IDS (Internal Design Specifications) which can be purchased from HP tell us that the bender is driven directly by the Saturn CPU. In any case, the August 1987 HP Journal gives many of these details. The connections to the right-hand hybrid look rather complicated, and it is turned at a right angle compared to the same chip in the HP-18C. It is simpler to study the connections to the left-hand hybrid (marked 1LP3-0016 in the HP-28C). Starting at its lower right hand corner and going counter-clockwise (up the right-hand edge) we find (after a great deal of effort, this information is NOT given in the HP Journal) that the pin connections are as follows:

1. B0 - Bus line 0
2. B1 - Bus line 1
3. B2 - Bus line 2
4. B3 - Bus line 3
5. *STR - signal strobe
6. Not connected

7. *CD - Command/Data selector
8. DIN - Daisy In
9. DO - Daisy Out
10.GND - Ground
11.VDD - Power supply

These are all the signals we need to use for connecting additional soft configured memory, so I shall stop there. All the other pins are connected to one of pins 8, 10 or 11, except for pin 28 which like pin 6 is not connected to anything. The daisy chain input line carries the signal which tells each chip's controller in turn to carry out the operations required to soft configure it, and the daisy chain output line passes this signal on to the next chip in sequence, once the chip has been configured. For those who are interested, pin 9 is connected to a lead which goes through the board and under the right hand display driver, but it is not clear that there is an electrical connection to the driver hybrid. The right hand hybrid does not have a separate daisy chain input line; as with port 1 of the HP-71B, its daisy chain input signal is connected to VDD, so it is always high. Its pin 9 also goes to the corresponding display driver; again there is no clear connection. The Saturn design allows for more than one daisy chain, the HP-28C seems to have two: one goes directly to the right hand hybrid, and from there to the display driver below. The other goes to the left hand hybrid and then to the driver below. The left hand hybrid has a clear daisy chain input signal, which we can safely use to configure one or two RAM chips which we build in.

5.6 What else is there? Before going on to explain how to connect the extra RAM, let me pause to describe a few other things. The infra-red transmitter bulb is the transparent object at the top right of photograph 3. It is connected to two signal lines, and there are two more connectors to its right: these are not for I/O as some people had hoped, they are just VDD and GND. The left-hand connector to the bulb is controlled through a transistor which amplifies the signal, if you have a sufficiently strong dislike of communicating with a printer by I-R then you could connect a printer directly via two wires attached to the right hand bulb connector and to the small pad at the left of the left hand bulb connector. You could even try using this to send data to another device. This is one modification that can be made to the HP-28S as well as the HP-28C. There is no easy way of using these lines to send anything TO the HP-28, but in principle that can be done, since the I/O line is a two-way line - it's just that there is no circuitry or software built in to receive inputs.

Instead of building an interface you can buy the Hook-uP made by RUSH systems and use it to send information to a PC, see Appendix B for details.

If you really wanted to interface your HP-28 to a microcomputer you could send data and programs from the HP-28 to the micro using the printer signals. Then you could send signals from the micro to the HP-28 through the 21 keyboard connectors along the bottom edge of the board. You would have to program the micro to interpret signals intended for the printer, and to translate anything it sends to the HP-28 into keystroke combinations - but this could be worthwhile if you add 64K RAM to an HP-28C and want to send out or read in a lot of programs or data. You could even set the HP-28 TRACE flag so your micro could use the printer output to tell when the HP-28 has finished with one set of keystrokes and is ready for the next.

Directly below the large capacitor at the top of the board and to the top left of the right-hand hybrid is a 180 milliHenry inductor. To its left are two capacitors used with the inductor to form an LC circuit. The components of this CPU timer circuit are laid out as in the diagram below:

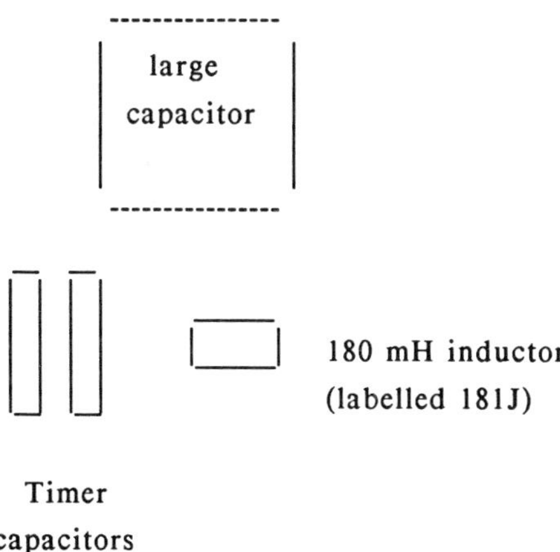

To speed up your HP-28C you need to replace the two smaller capacitors with lower valued ones. These should be surface-mount capacitors; 10 pF speeds up the HP-28C to about 180% of its normal speed - very useful, particularly if you add extra RAM to it - the extra RAM speeds up some operations but garbage collection takes longer and a speed-up makes this less annoying. Nearly all HP-28Cs will work at this higher speed, if yours refuses to work then try another pair of 10pF capacitors (you may have a cracked cap!), but if that still does not work then you will have to go back to higher values. Most HP-28Cs will work at even higher speeds, but the printer will not work with them at these higher speeds. The HP-28S has a different timer circuit - the capacitors are not at all easily accessible, and in any case the HP-28S already runs at 1MHz, so there is less reason to try speeding it up.

You may wonder why there is a timer circuit of this sort if the HP-28 has a crystal oscillator built in. The crystal oscillator is used to provide an accurate 32.768 kHz signal to control the clock and other functions such as timing of signals to the printer. The LC circuit described above provides a clock rate of about 617 kHz, for the HP-28C CPU. The design of the CPU and internal data bus allows them to operate at up to 1 MHz (greater speeds are usually possible but outside the design limits), so a speed-up as described works on most HP-28Cs. During printing the HP-28 uses the crystal oscillator to calibrate the CPU timer to get an accurate timing for signals sent to the printer; the calibration instructions allow for variations in the LC clock from one HP-28 to another, but they do not allow for too high a speed, such as that generated by the LC circuit when the capacitor values are much below 10pF. Thus the printer will work with an HP-28S or an HP-28C speeded up to 1MHz, but not much faster.

I would not like to risk doing anything else with my HP-28, but don't let me stop you trying. One thing worth trying is to use the I/O line from the other display driver as an input line. If you learn anything more, do write it up for a user club journal!

5.7 Adding the RAM. OK, we are nearly ready to add in the extra RAM. If you plan to remove some RAM from an HP-71B plug-in 4K or larger module, then first break open the module. You can force it open from the front by pushing in a wide-bladed knife and twisting it sideways, or by pushing in a pair of thin-nosed pliers and then forcing them open. It does not matter if you damage the gold-plated contacts, as you will not be using them again, but be very careful not to damage the small board itself. Once you have taken this out, unsolder the gold-plated contacts. Solder wick or some other solder remover is better than just applying heat and pulling. Tidy up the board, removing any unwanted solder. The 4K RAM board should now look something like photograph 4, though it will not look exactly the same. There are 13 connectors, starting from the left (with the board lying circuit side up as in the photograph); here is what each one is and what it should be connected to on the left hand hybrid on the HP-28C board:

1. GND - ground, connect to pin 10 on hybrid
2. *INT - do not use
3. OD - do not use
4. IR14 - do not use
5. DO - see notes below
6. DIN - daisy chain input, connect to pin 8 on hybrid
7. *CD - connect to pin 7
8. *STR - connect to pin 5
9. B3 - connect to pin 4
10. B2 - connect to pin 3
11. B1 - connect to pin 2
12. B0 - connect to pin 1
13. VDD - connect to pin 11

Connector 5 is the daisy chain output signal. If you are putting only one RAM board into your HP-28C then you can leave this unconnected. If you are putting in two boards then connect this connector from the first board to connector 6 on the second board. That way you will have a configuration daisy chain going from pin 8 on the 1LP3-0016 hybrid to connector 6 on the first board, and then from connector 5 on the first board to connector 6 on the second board. In this case, leave connector 5 of the second board unconnected. It may be wiser to connect a second RAM board to the right hand hybrid in the HP-28C, in that case you must note that pins 1 to 11 of this hybrid lie along its bottom edge, starting at the left hand end.

If you use a CMT 32K RAM board then the order of connectors should be the same if you place the board with the circuit face up (i.e. with the components facing down, towards the surface on which the board is lying). Some people have told me that they got confused when they tried this, because they had the PCB lying component side up. I have also heard claims that the four data lines B0 to B3 are in the opposite order on 4K RAM boards. If your HP-28C refuses to show a meaningful display after you have connected up the RAM, but does turn on (the display dots can be seen when the HP-28C is viewed from an angle) then you may need to reverse the data line connections or all the connections, as mentioned two paragraphs down.

All the connections from the RAM board to the hybrid in the HP-28C should be made with very fine insulated wire (30 gauge would be sensible) using a temperature controlled narrow-tipped soldering pencil. Remember you will be soldering directly to CMOS chips! Use fairly short pieces of wire, but long enough that you can reach a suitable space for the extra RAM board or boards you are putting into your HP-28C. It is quite difficult to fit the extra board into the confined space in the HP-28C, particularly the 32K RAM unit. A good place is directly below the infra-red bulb; you have to cut out some of the reinforcing plastic in that area but the board will replace that. With a RAM unit like this replacing the reinforcing plastic the HP-28C is bound to be less well able to withstand shocks such as being dropped, so be careful with it! Once you have connected up the board or boards, put them into the space you have made, make sure there is no risk of any cross-contacts (use some insulation if necessary), and attach the board or boards firmly. Use a non-corrosive adhesive or silicone compound designed for holding together printed circuit boards (PCBs) or double-sided tape; do not use ordinary glues since many of them can corrode a PCB.

If you used sticky tape to hold together the keyboard then you should be able to replace the circuit and keyboard in the case without using glue. You should then be able to install the batteries and do a MEM without putting together your HP-28C. If nothing happens, check the batteries are in the right way and are firmly connected. Then check all your solder joints, check the connections have been made as described and check for any shorts. If the connections seem to be good but nothing happens then you may have all of the pins 1 - 13 in reverse order, or you may have the data lines 0 - 4 in reverse order. Try changing one or both - a total of four possible combinations. If things still fail to work then remove the RAM entirely and check again - if the HP-28C refuses to work then you have probably left some solder on the board and this is short circuiting something. Check the board, then try again. If your HP-28C is still dead then bad luck! You may be able to find some short circuit or some damage, otherwise you will probably have to go out and buy a new HP-28! Be more careful next time! As a last resort, check if there is an expert in your local user group who might help you.

Once everything is working you can put the case together - be sure none of your wires are trapped or pressed together in such a way that a short can occur or that the insulation might wear through. Make sure as well that nothing is touching the bender, otherwise you are likely to hear some very odd BEEPs. If any keys have come loose hold the keyboard upside down and put all the keys back in. This needs some care to make sure all the keys end up in the right places. Push the back onto the keyboard, turn the whole thing over, and use something to hold it together temporarily while you insert the batteries and again check that everything is working. Now you can reattach the keyboard to the back case, using some suitable material to replace the drilled-out peg tops - better still use a warm soldering iron to melt the remains of the pegs back over the front of the keyboard. If you ever decide to re-open the case it may be very difficult to drill it out and replace it again, so I suggest you close only a few holes at first, until you are sure the memory extension works and you do not want to make any more changes. Then you can fill in all the holes. Finally, reattach the overlays on the keyboard and above the display. You should now have an HP-28C which looks as good as new but actually is better than new, since it has more user memory!

Well, that's what is inside an HP-28, and what you can add to it, particularly to an HP-28C. This information has been confirmed by Kim Holm, in Denmark, and several other user group members. Kim Holm in Denmark, and David White (via EduCALC, see Appendix A) in California will add RAM for you if you do not want to take the risk yourself. The extra memory will let you store more programs and data in your HP-28C; it will also let you do things such as Taylor expansions with more terms. The HP-28C remains a calculator though, for example 32K extra RAM lets you expand 'EXP(SIN(X)) to 7 terms instead of a maximum of 4 with a normal HP-28C but the 4th order expansion takes 30 seconds whereas the 7th order one takes 3800 seconds! Even 32K extra is not enough to go to the 8th order.

The information here has come from a variety of sources. A great deal of it was gleaned from studying the HPCC club project HP-28C. Many thanks to Colin Crowther for providing the HP-28C before there was enough money in the fund to pay for it, and many thanks to all who contributed to the fund. Rabin Ezra took the HP-28C apart, with Mark Cracknell and myself looking over his shoulder; Ian Maw made helpful suggestions. Graeme and Roger at Zengrange took apart the little pieces left by Rabin into littler pieces and did the electrical tests.   Jeremy Smith provided spare components. (The photographs of the HP-28C are mine.) While examining the HP-28C and writing this I learned a lot from the HP-71B Internal Documentation Set, of which I own a copy, and from the articles about the HP-71 Memory System by Jim De Arras in CHHU Chronicle V1N1 and in the proceedings of the 1985 Atlanta HP Handheld Conference. My thanks also to Kim Holm for testing out my original 4K RAM expansion ideas on his HP-28C. (Yes, I have done a 32K RAM expansion myself too.) The August and October 1987 HP Journals came out too late to help with the original research, but provided additional interesting information - do read them if you want to learn more about the HP-28 hardware.

* * *

5.8 Customizing HP-28S and HP-28C menus. The HP-28S has a new internal design and its software has been rewritten, so extra memory cannot be built in. As it has 32K bytes of RAM already in it and runs at 1MHz this should not worry owners, at least not until HP introduce something even better! 32K of RAM is a lot of memory for a calculator, and could be used to store over 3000 variables. That would make 500 USER menus! The designers very sensibly provided the HP-28S with some extra commands to control the USER menu, in particular to split it up into submenus or subdirectories. You can customize your HP-28S very effectively by using subdirectories, but this requires an understanding of how they work and some planning of their use. This point makes some suggestions on the subject; in the next point I shall show how submenus can be created on an HP-28C too - this should be of particular interest to people who have added extra memory to an HP-28C.

Here is a figure to show one possible way of laying out the USER menu and submenus on an HP-28S. I shall use this layout to explain some important features of HP-28S menus.

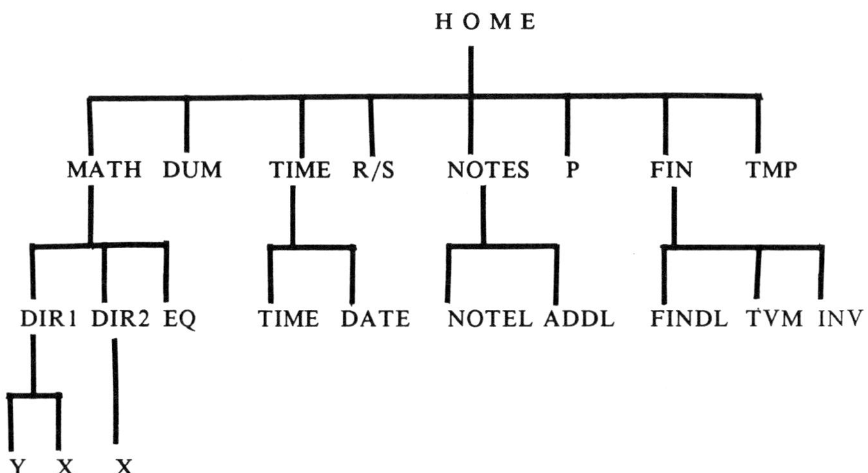

1. If you execute HOME then the USER menu will show the variables on the line below HOME in the layout. The six names MATH, DUM, TIME, R/S, NOTES, and P will be visible in the display, the two other names FIN and TMP will not be visible unless you use NEXT to move to them. These eight variables are said to be in the "home directory", or "top-level directory".

2. If you now execute MATH, TIME, NOTES or FIN then you will move down into one of these "subdirectories" on the second level, and the display will show the corresponding "submenu". For example if you type MATH or press the menu key labelled MATH then the display will show two menu labels with the names DIR1 and DIR2; the other menu labels will be blank, but of course you could have more variables in the MATH subdirectory, and they would then show up in the menu as well. If you had more than six variables in the MATH subdirectory, then you would need to use NEXT to see beyond the first six. The other variables in the HOME directory are not subdirectories. DUM is a "dummy" which is just there to make sure R/S is at the far

right. If you use a dummy variable like this, then store an empty text string in it to use the least possible amount of RAM. R/S is the Run/Stop name which I described in point 3.10 - if you want to use such a program then it should clearly be in the first part of the USER menu, at the right hand end as I described. P is a useful program which I shall describe below - it has to be in the home directory so it can be used from any subdirectory. TMP is a variable created to store some temporary object.

3. The MATH subdirectory contains the equation EQ and two more subdirectories DIR1 and DIR2. You can move down to either of these - they both contain the variable X. As is described in Chapter 4 of the Owner's manual, this allows you to have two different values of X - but EQ is one directory level higher, so you can move to either DIR1 or DIR2 and use different values of X, yet the same equation.

4. Note that EQ is in a directory directly above either X, so you can use EQ from either of the subdirectories DIR1 and DIR2. You could also use P or TMP, because they are both in a directory directly above DIR1 and DIR2 - they are inside a directory in the "current path". If you are in DIR1, then the current path is the list of directories { HOME MATH DIR1 }; EQ is in MATH, UP and TMP are in HOME. On the other hand, the variable NTS is not in the current path - if you type the name 'NTS' while you are in DIR1 or DIR2 or MATH then the name will not be found and will be treated as a symbolic variable. This is clearly necessary; if variables in all other directories were available then 'X' would be ambiguous, since it could refer to 'X' either in DIR1 or DIR2. Equally, 'X' can not be found while you are in any directory above it, since that could again be ambiguous - if you were in the HOME directory then 'X' could refer to either of the variables in DIR1 or DIR2; instead the HP-28S is designed so no variable in any subdirectory below the current one can be found until you move down to that directory.

5. An interesting result of this is that you can also have the same name used two times one above the other, as with the subdirectory called TIME containing a program called TIME. If you are in DIR1

then you can execute TIME, and this will evaluate TIME in the HOME directory (in the current path), putting you in the TIME subdirectory. Now if you execute TIME again then the HP-28S will search the new current path { HOME TIME } and will find the variable TIME inside the TIME subdirectory, which has become the "current directory". In the example layout given here, the TIME subdirectory contains several programs related to time calculations, and the TIME program finds the present time (see point 3.2). To get the present time while you are in DIR1 you would do TIME TIME.

6. If you are in the DIR1 subdirectory and you want to move back up to MATH then you have to type MATH - but what if you forget which subdirectory you are in and which one is above it? You can use HOME to get back to the top level, and then move back down to MATH, but this is rather cumbersome. Alternatively you can use PATH to find out where you are, then pick the second-from-last name and evaluate it - but this is rather awkward too. The designers really should have provided an UP command to let you move up by one subdirectory level from wherever you are. The program UP given among the programming examples at the end of the Owner's manual will let you move up one or more levels, but it is not the simple one-up command that most users need most of the time. What is really needed is a command that is available at all times from the keyboard, with a minimum of fuss. An obvious place to put this command would be the shifted P key, since this is the only unused key on the HP-28S keyboard. (Maybe the designers plan to use it for some special purpose on a future HP-28 model - perhaps even an I/O menu?) I suggest the following program which will move you up by one level from any subdirectory:

```
<< PATH       ;use PATH to get a list of directories in the current
              ;path
   DUP SIZE   ;find number of directories in this list
   1 -        ;calculate position of the next directory up in this
              ;list
   1 MAX      ;if you are in HOME then you cannot go up - replace 0
              ;with 1
```

>   GET >>   ;get the name of this directory to level 1 of the
>   ;stack

HOME 'P' STO;store this program in the HOME directory with the
>   ;name 'P'

To move up from any subdirectory to the one above you can now press
P EVAL. As mentioned above, I think the shifted P key would be the
ideal key for this command - using P EVAL is the closest I could
get. If you are already in the HOME directory then PATH DUP SIZE 1
- gives the result 0, and GET gives an error, so I use 1 MAX which
is a very quick way to replace 0 with 1 under these conditions -
this causes HOME to be executed, which has no effect if you are
already in the home directory. You may prefer to put EVAL after GET
in the program, so you could use P ENTER from the keyboard or just P
in a program, but as the program stands you can use P ENTER to see
the name of the directory above the current one or P EVAL to get to
that directory - with two keystrokes for either operation.

7. This 'P' command will only work in all directories if you put it
in the HOME directory; if you put some other variable called 'P' in
a subdirectory then this command will not work while that other P is
in the current path. If there is no other P in the current path
then the P command will be found from the home directory or from any
subdirectory. This means that P is a "global variable" - one which
can be found by any program or subprogram, as opposed to a
"local variable" which can only be used by a program or subroutine
which knows of that variable. Details of local variables were given
in point 2.14. On an HP-28C there is only one USER menu, so all
variables that are not local are automatically global. On the HP-
28S there can be variables in subdirectories, and these are not
truly "global" - chapter 16 of the HP-28S Owner's manual says that
all variables are either local or otherwise global - but I suggest
that non-local variables should be called "ordinary variables" if
they are not in the home directory. One more sort of name; some
ordinary variables are "temporary variables" - a few commands create
a temporary user variable, for example DRAW creates a variable whose

name is the name of the independent plot variable. If DRAW (or INTEGRATE, QUAD, TAYLR) is aborted by a System Halt or by Out of Memory then the temporary variable is not deleted, so more than one copy of a variable with the same name can be created. The HP-28C Reference manual points out that PURGE can be used to delete such duplicate variables, the HP-28S manuals do not mention them, but the same comments apply.

8. The layout of the HOME directory in this example shows how the HP-28S can be customized to behave like a pocket computer - with one menu for mathematical work, a second menu for time and date operations, a third menu for making notes or lists, and a fourth one for financial calculations. Many pocket computers such as the HP-41CX or the Psion Organizer provide all these features; the use of subdirectories lets you add these features as a set of options on the HP-28S. Programs to let you set up notes or lists on the HP-28S will be described in point 5.10. The one thing you cannot do on an HP-28S (except with a lot of machine language programming) is set up alarms and reminders. There again, you can customize your HP-28S by setting up more subdirectories for special mathematical work which would be more difficult or impossible on other models.

5.9 Subdirectories for the HP-28C. The HP-28C does not have subdirectories as such, but look at the following layout of a customized HP-28C USER menu:

MATH	TIME	FIN	MENU	DUM	R/S
Y	X	EQ	D0	D1	D2
TIM	DATE	D3	D4	D5	D6
TVM	INV	D7	D8	D9	DA
NXT	TMP				

The top line shows the first six variables which would show up in the first part of the USER menu. The next line shows the next six, and so on. This layout is very similar to that shown in the previous point. I have left out the NOTES, for which there would not be enough room (unless you make very few notes or add some extra RAM); I have put in the MENU program from point 3.11 instead. I have also replaced the "up" program by the "next" program from point 3.11. The variable MATH should be the program << NXT >>, the variable TIME should be << NXT NXT >>, and the variable FIN should be << NXT NXT NXT >>. This way, pressing MATH moves you to the maths menu which contains X, Y and EQ, TIME moves you to the TIME menu, and FIN moves you to the finance menu. Pressing USER returns you to the "home" menu.

Setting up these menus takes more effort than on the HP-28S because you have to group everything in sixes. As with the HP-28S example there is a dummy variable in the main menu, but now we need the additional dummy variables D0 to DA which are required to set everything up in groups of six. Since the HP-28C has less RAM than the HP-28S and since we need more dummy variables it is important to make every dummy as short as possible by storing the empty text string "" in each one. If something goes wrong, or you decide to add some extra variables then you can use ORDER to rearrange the variables. One problem is that 'R/S' is a "synthetic" or Non-Normalized name, so if you want to use ORDER to move such a name around then you will need to have a copy of the name, as described in point 3.10.

This can be a very useful customization of the HP-28C, let us add one last neat touch. As you can see, I have changed the name of the TIME program to TIM, as it is not normally possible to have two variables with the same name. You can, however, create a variable called TIME and store the time program in it, then create a duplicate variable called TIME, as described in part 7 of the previous point. Do this by plotting an equation called 'SIN(TIME)' and interrupting the drawing with a System Halt (ON UP). Now you will have a second variable called TIME as well, and you will be able to store the program << NXT NXT >> in the new copy. One problem is that you will have to position the first copy correctly with ORDER before creating the second copy.

5.10 An electronic notebook. An electronic notebook holds a list of items such as notes to yourself, or names and telephone numbers. The advantage of an electronic notebook is that you can use programs to look for names or notes, instead of having to read through the whole list yourself when you look for a particular name or note. In this point I shall show how you can customize an HP-28S with four programs to make it work like an electronic notebook. The first program adds a new note to a list called NOTEL; if the list does not exist yet then the program creates it. The second program lets you look for a specified item in the list. The third lets you continue looking further down the list to see if an item occurs a second or further time. If you wish you can modify the programs to use more than one list, and you can add other programs (the fourth program is an example of this, showing how you can write a program to delete items from the list), or to sort the list (an example of a SORT program is given as one of the examples in the HP-28S Owner's Manual). The programs will need to be modified to work on an HP-28C, but that does not really have enough memory to be used as an electronic notebook unless you have extended its memory as described earlier in this chapter.

The notes will be held in a list called NOTEL (this stands for NOTE List, but you can think of it as TELephone NOs. too). If the list is to contain names and telephone numbers then each item can be a text string with a name and a number in it; you could include addresses too, and in that case you should keep each name and address in one string but separate the name and lines in the address with NEWLINEs - type ", then the name, then NEWLINE, then the first line of the address, then another NEWLINE, and so on. The list does not have to be made up of text strings though; for example you could put exam marks in it, then look to see if a particular mark is in the list. You can even mix different types of objects in the list. A program called ADDL (ADD to List) will be used to add new notes or other items to the list, but you can edit the list and add items to it in some other way if you wish. ADDL will add new items to the front of the list - this is not the normal way lists are used, but the newest items are often the ones you look for most often so it is sensible to have them at the front - then it will take less time to find them than if they were to be at the end.

To find a particular item in the list we shall use the program FINDL - but this will only find the first time a given object shows up in the list. An extra program called CONTL (CONTinue Looking) will be used to look if the same item shows up again in the list. (In fact FINDL uses CONTL to find the first time an item occurs in the list.) FINDL and CONTL will look for complete objects (say the number 75 in a list of exam marks), but if the object is a text string then they will also look at every text string in the list to see if the text string is part of a string in the list. For example looking for the text string "CHR" will find all of the strings in the list { "CHRISTINE 999-7940" "CHRIS" "REMEMBER CHRISTMAS GIFTS" }. If you look for "CHRIS" then "CHRIS" will be found by FINDL (because FINDL first looks for complete objects which match) and then CONTL will find "REMEMBER CHRISTMAS GIFTS". Christine's telephone number will not be found - to look for it you should use FINDL to look for the string "CHR".

As I suggested in point 5.8, the list and all the programs should be kept in a separate subdirectory, called something like NOTES. Create this subdirectory, go into it, and type in the program ADDL.

ADDL.

    object in level 1 -> object removed from stack, added to NOTEL list.

```
<<
    DUP DROP            ;First check for an entry on the stack
    RCLF SWAP 31 CF     ;Save present flags, clear LAST flag needed
                        ;for IFERR
    IF DUP TYPE 5 ==    ;If the object to add is a list, use ->STR
    THEN ->STR "{"      ;and STR-> to put it inside a second list
      SWAP + STR->      ;(a useful trick!), so that + will put the
```

```
END                      ;new list inside NOTEL instead of adding it
                         ;to NOTEL
IFERR 'NOTEL' RCL        ;If NOTEL does not exist (RCL cannot find it)
THEN { }                 ;then create an empty list - the LAST flag
END                      ;must be clear so an error will drop the
                         ;name 'NOTEL'
+                        ;Add new object to NOTEL or the empty list
'NOTEL' STO              ;Store the new list in NOTEL
STOF                     ;Restore the original flag status
>>


'ADDL' STO               ;Store the program in the variable ADDL
```

To try the program out, type "REMEMBER CHRISTMAS GIFTS, then press
ENTER, and then ADDL. Observe that the new name NOTEL appears in
the USER menu. Repeat this for the strings "CHRIS" and Christine's
telephone number. Now press NOTEL to bring the whole list to the
stack, and use EDIT to see the whole of each line in the list (this
is when NEWLINEs can be of help).

Next type in the program FINDL:

```
FINDL
                    object to be found, position in list
                    (if the whole object is found)

                /
object to be found in list  -> object to be found, 0  (if not found at all)
                \
                    string containing the object looked for,
                    position in list (if object to find is a
                    a string, and the whole string is not found,
                    but a longer string containing the object is)

<<
'OBJL' STO       ;Store object to look for in variable OBJL
0 'POSL' STO     ;Store 0 as position where OBJL was last found
CONTL            ;Use CONTL to continue looking, from the list front
>>
```

```
'FINDL' STO          ;Store the program
```

Note that the object to be found is stored in OBJL so it can be used again, and the position where it was most recently found is stored in POSL. Now we must type in the program CONTL. It will do two things, first look for OBJL in that part of NOTEL which has not yet been examined, using the HP-28S ability of POS to see if the object in level 1 matches any of the objects in the list in level 2. If OBJL is not found this way, then CONTL will call a separate program SRCHL to search the remaining part of NOTEL for a character string which matches OBJL. If you do not want this search for character strings then replace DROP SRCHL at the end with 'POSL' STO DROP OBJL 0, and ignore the part about SRCHL.

CONTL
    -> return object and position, as defined for POSL

```
<<
  NOTEL                  ;Get the full list
  POSL 1 +               ;Get position of 1st object not yet checked
  OVER SIZE              ;Position of last object to check is list size
  SUB DUP               ;Get sub-list still to be searched, need a
                         ;duplicate
    OBJL POS            ;See if the whole OBJL can be found in it
    IF DUP             ;If so then add position in sublist to previous
    THEN 'POSL' STO+   ;position to get new POSL, then drop
      DROP OBJL POSL   ;remaining copy of sublist, put OBJL and
                       ;POSL on stack and finish
    ELSE DROP SRCHL    ;If not found drop the 0 and call SRCHL to
    END                ;look for OBJL within each character string
                       ;in the sublist
>>
```

```
'CONTL' STO          ;Store the program
```

If the whole list has already been searched then SUB will get an empty list but POS will accept that. We still have to type in the program SRCHL before we can do anything. In principle SRCHL could be included as part of CONTL, but that would make CONTL 89 steps long, which is uncomfortably long, particularly if you are looking for a bug or a typing error.

SRCHL

        object searched for, 0

        (if object not found or is not a string)

 sublist to search ->

        string containing search string, position in NOTEL

        (if found)

```
<<
   RCLF SWAP 31 CF          ;Save flags, clear flag 35 so IFERR
                            ;drops objects
   IF DUP SIZE              ;Check sublist size (may be empty)
   OBJL TYPE 2 == AND       ;then check that OBJL is a character
                            ;string, both must be true
   THEN 1 1                 ;If so then start GETI index at 1, get
                            ;spare copy
     DO DROP                ;DO..WHILE to check list, drop previous
                            ;result
       GETI                 ;Get next list element
       IFERR OBJL POS       ;See if OBJL is in it (error if not a
                            ;string) -
       THEN 0               ;if an error then answer is 0 anyway
       END                  ;This element checked, result 0 if not
                            ;found
     UNTIL OVER 1 ==        ;To finish DO..WHILE the GETI index
       OVER OR              ;must be back at 1 or POS result must
                            ;be non-zero
     END                    ;If result of OR is not 1 then repeat
                            ;DO loop
     IF                     ;Otherwise loop finished, check if
                            ;OBJL found
     THEN 1 -               ;Yes - position in sub-list is GETI
       IF DUP NOT           ;index -1 but if this is zero then it
```

```
    THEN DROP DUP SIZE   ;was at the last position, so position
                         ;is sublist size instead
    END                  ;Position checked, get corresponding
  SWAP OVER GET SWAP     ;string from other copy of sublist and
                         ;put position in level 1
  ELSE DROP2 OBJL 0      ;Loop finished, OBJL not found, put in
                         ;OBJL and 0
    END                  ;End THEN clause if OBJL was a
                         ;character string
  ELSE DROP OBJL 0       ;Otherwise put OBJL and 0 again
  END                    ;End of search
  'POSL'                 ;Put name of 'POSL' on stack
  IF OVER                ;If a result was found (position is not
  THEN STO+              ;0), then add it to POSL,
  ELSE STO               ;otherwise store a 0 in POSL
  END POSL ROT STOF      ;End check, get position from POSL,
                         ;restore flags
>>

'SRCHL' STO              ;Store the program SeaRch for
                         ;CHaracters in List
```

At last we can check the programs. First of all, double check that
the programs in your HP-28S are exactly the same as above. Now type
"CHRIS, press ENTER, then press FINDL. FINDL will store "CHRIS" as
the object to be found, and 0 as the address where it was last
found. CONTL will then look for the whole string "CHRIS" in the
list, and will tell you it found the string "CHRIS" at position 2 in
the list. The position 2 will now be stored in POSL, and if you
press CONTL then it will continue the search, beginning at object 3
in the list (in this case that is the last object in the list, so
the sub-list to be searched contains only 1 object, but this need
not be so). CONTL will not find "CHRIS" in the list, so it will
call SRCHL to search the list for the character string "CHRIS"
inside other character strings. "CHRIS" will be found in the
remaining object in the list, so the whole item will be put in
level 2, and its position in the list will be put in level 1. If

you want to read the whole of the string, drop the value from level 1 and EDIT the string, or VISIT the string in level 2. If the string is a name and address, then including NEWLINEs in it (as suggested earlier) will make sure each line of the address is on a separate line in the display when you EDIT or VISIT it, so the address will be easier to read.

The programs have not found Christine! If you press CONTL again then you will see "CHRIS" in level 2, and 0 in level 1, telling you no more copies of "CHRIS" were found. If you press CONTL yet again then the program starts over from the beginning, and finds "CHRIS" at position 2 in the list again. To find Christine, you must look for the text string "CHR" - this does not match any complete object in the list so it will be searched for in every text string, from the beginning of the list. The programs are "case-sensitive" - this means that they know the difference between upper case and lower case letters, so looking for "Chris" will not find anything in this example. Changing from upper case to lower case and back again is a bit awkward on the HP-28, so most people will use upper case letters only in their notes and in the strings to be looked for; you can rewrite the programs to turn all strings into upper case first if you need.

Maybe we should get rid of that annoying "CHRIS" in the list! Use "CHRIS" FINDL to find this text string again. Its position is now stored in POSL as well as being on the stack. This is very useful - to remove the unwanted value we need only make up two new lists, one containing all the values before that marked by POSL, the other containing all the values after POSL. Then we can add these two sub-lists together and the result is the original list, but with the unwanted value deleted. Type in this program:

DELL

      Deletes value at position POSL from list in NOTEL, stack unchanged.

```
<<
   NOTEL                    ;Bring a copy of the list to the stack
   1 POSL 1 -               ;Start at position 1, end 1 before POSL
   SUB                      ;Create this sub-list
   NOTEL                    ;Get another copy of the whole list
   POSL 1 + OVER SIZE       ;Start 1 past POSL, end at list end (its size)
   SUB                      ;Create this second sub-list
   +                        ;Add the two sub-lists together
   'NOTEL' STO              ;Store the new list in NOTEL
>>
```

```
'DELL' STO                  ;Store the program "DELete List item"
```

Compared to some of the earlier programs this is very easy - you can write other programs for yourself using OBJL and POSL. (For example DELL can be modified to replace the item at POSL instead of deleting it.) Now delete "CHRIS" from the list simply by pressing DELL. To check this has happened, press NOTEL to bring a copy to the stack. DELL can delete the first and last items of a list; if POSL is less than 1 or greater than the list size then the list will be unchanged, as required. Some of the things that HP-28 commands do may seem odd, until you write a program like this and see that the action of the commands naturally gives the results you want - clever design!

Now that you have checked the programs, try a different example. PURGE the list NOTEL, and use ADDL to build up a list of exam marks for a class in which the students had the marks 41, 49, 53, 58, 64, 69, 75, 75, 79, 83. Use ADDL to add each mark to the list. Did anyone get 50% - press 50 FINDL; the answer is that 50 was not found. Did anyone get 75% - press 75 FINDL - and see that the third student got 75%. Did any more students get this mark? Press CONTL and see that the fourth one did as well. Any more? Pressing CONTL again will give the answer no. This is a simple use of the electronic notebook for something other than names; you could instead have made a list of character strings with each student's name and mark.

This brings us to the end, except for the Appendices. I hope that the ideas in this book have shown how versatile your HP-28 is, and how you can customize it to your own needs. If you have been keeping a notebook then go over it and make a shorter list of the ideas you want to use in future. If you have not been keeping a notebook, maybe you will go back to the beginning and use the HP-28S notebook programs to make notes for yourself. Then, if you have a problem, you will be able to type in the name of the command giving the trouble, and use FINDL to find any notes about the command. If you have a printer then you can print out the whole list, but printing is a separate topic not covered here - to find out more look in Appendix A for other books about the HP-28, or join a club.

APPENDIX A – FURTHER SOURCES OF INFORMATION AND EQUIPMENT

This Appendix lists sources of information about the HP-28, and equipment for it, including shops and organizations that provide such information. First of all, the HP-28 comes with two manuals. A booklet of programming examples was included with HP-28Cs sold after about October 1987. Before then HP produced a different set of examples which were sent to people asking HP for help. A description of how SYSEVAL can be used to access the system clock has been published by HP under the title "HP-28C Solutions 28-1", which implies that more Solutions like this might be published. Four Step-by-Step example booklets for the HP-28C and S have been published by Hewlett-Packard - "Algebra and College Math", "Calculus", "Probability and Statistics" and "Vectors and Matrices", plus "Electrical Engineering" for the HP-28S. All contain examples which help explain the use of HP-28 commands, and the fourth includes an extended example showing how matrices can be used in a suite of programs for forest management and harvesting calculations. The August 1987 Hewlett-Packard Journal (Vol. 38, No. 8) was devoted to hardware and software descriptions of the HP-18C and HP-28C, with further information on the printer, the interface to the printer and manufacturing methods in the October 1987 HP Journal (Vol. 38, No. 10). Previous HP Journals have had information on the Saturn CPU, see especially the July 1984 issue (Vol. 35, No. 7).

All of the above information relates directly to the HP-28 and is available straight from HP. (I am told that more information is sometimes published in HP internal journals but these are not released outside HP.) Another source of information from HP is provided by various publications on the HP-71B, in particular the HP-71B Internal Design Specification (IDS) - a collection of documents describing the hardware, software, and peripherals. They are sold at a high price to deter ordinary users from buying them, while allowing software and hardware companies to buy them and design new items for use with the HP-71B. For HP-28 use the most relevant document, and the least expensive, is volume 1 of the

Software IDS - it describes the Saturn CPU machine language and most of the relevant system information. One extra IDS volume - for the FORTH/Assembler ROM - has been published by the user club CHHU. This club has closed down but members of other clubs may still be able to contact Richard Nelson to ask for a copy, or they may find a copy in their club library. Some of the same information is in the FORTH/Assembler ROM Owner's Manual; the information is relevant because HP-28 RPL is very similar to the HP-71B implementation of FORTH.

Some of the HP-28 mathematical functions are taken from the HP-71B Math Pac and from the HP-15C. The manual for the HP-71B Math Pac can provide some useful ideas, and the "HP-15C Advanced Functions Handbook" has many of the advanced details that HP-28 users may want but cannot find in the Reference Manual. This "Handbook" gives detailed explanations of matrix operations, and the best discussion of numerical accuracy on calculators I have ever seen. It is to be hoped that HP will produce a similar handbook for the HP-28, in the meantime I would urge serious users to consider buying the HP-15C version. Some of this information (and a great deal more!) is now available in the book "HP-28 Insights - Principles and Programming of the HP-28C/S" by Dr. Bill Wickes, leader of the HP-28 design team, list price $25 plus postage, available from Larken Publications, 4517 NW Queens Ave., Corvallis OR 97330, USA, and from bookstores, including EduCALC, see below.

Two other books about the HP-28 are "An Easy Course in Using the HP-28C" and an update - "An Easy Course in Using the HP-28S", both by John W. Loux and Chris Coffin, published by Grapevine Publications. The first book was written when only the HP-28C was available, the second one mentions the HP-28S by name, but nearly all of it relates equally well to the HP-28C, and some of the Appendices in the first book have been expanded into extra chapters in the second one, so it is 82 pages longer. The books have many drawings and cartoons - the authors make it quite clear that the books are "an easy course", particularly for people who find the HP manuals difficult. Books of tips and suggestions for other calculators can give you useful ideas, in particular books for the HP-41, and general RPN books, such as "Algorithms for RPN Calculators" by John A. Ball (1978) published by John Wiley & Sons, Inc. A list of other books about the HP-41 and RPN calculators in general is given in Appendix A of my book "Extend your HP-41" (1985) published by SYNTHETIX, P.O. Box 1080, Berkeley, CA 94701, U.S.A. "The BASIC HP-71" by Richard Harvey contains a description of Saturn machine language. All of these books can be ordered for you by shops and bookstores which specialize in HP calculators. If there are none near you then try EduCALC Mail Store, 27953 Cabot Road, Laguna Niguel, CA 92677, U.S.A. who sell all these books and print a list of products, over 100 pages long, several times a year. They accept credit card orders from the U.S.A. or overseas by telephone and will send you their list if you ask for one. They also provide extra RAM for the HP-28C and sell leather cases for the HP-28.

EduCALC also sell a stand for the HP-28, with a built-in infra-red receiver and a cable to send the signals to a serial port on a personal computer. Anything that could go to the printer is sent to a personal computer instead by this stand - program listings (to print), numbers and other data (to analyze further), even graphics (to plot). This unit is called the Hook-uP and comes with a floppy disk containing MS-DOS software to control reception of the signals. It costs about $80 and is made by RUSH Systems, P. O. Box 723, Bethel, CT 06801, USA.

Further information is best obtained from user clubs. This book is a follow-on to a regular HP-28 column I write for DATAFILE, the journal of the British club, HPCC. HP-28 information has also been published by the U.S. club HPX, in the Australian journal Technical Notes, and by user clubs in Belgium, Denmark, Holland, Finland and France. The Notes from the Copenhagen 1987 International HP Handheld Computer Users' Conference published by PPC-Denmark have a lot on the HP-28. Detailed information on the Saturn CPU has been published in the journals of PPC, PPC-Paris, and the (no longer active) Dutch group "Users Group Twente". A list of club addresses is given below. User clubs are often run by just a few active members, so the quality of their publications can change when a few members leave or join, and their addresses can change too. When writing to user clubs, put a return address on your letter (so it can be returned if need be) and if you write to one club and receive no reply, try another one - all will understand a letter in English.

UK and other European Countries

HPCC,
Geggs Lodge,
Hempton Road,
Deddington,
Oxon OX5 4QG,
United Kingdom

PPC-Denmark,
c/o Steen Petersen,
Gl. Landevej 19,
DK-2620 Albertslund,
Denmark

PCX,
Postbus 205,
B-8000 Brugge 1,
Belgium

HP-GC,
Quellijnstraat 47-3,
1072 XP Amsterdam,
The Netherlands

STAK,
c/o Tapani Tarvainen,
Yliopistonkatu 10 B 21,
SF-40100 Jyvaskyla,
Finland

CHHU-IT,
c/o Stefano Tendon,
Cantone delle Asse 5,
29100 Piacenza,
Italy

PPC-Paris,
BP 604,
75028 Paris Cedex 01,
France

CCD e.V.,
P.O. Box 110411,
Schwalbacherstr. 50 Hhs.,
D-6000 Frankfurt 1,
West Germany

AUSTRALIA

PPPM Inc.,
P.O. Box 512,
Ringwood, Vic. 3134,
Australia

CHHU Sydney,
C/- K. Besley,
Charlie Business Services,
22 Elsie Street,
Burwood, N.S.W. 2134,
Australia

USA/International

HPX,
P.O. Box 56627,
Atlanta, GA 30356,
U.S.A.

PPC,
P.O. Box 90579,
Long Beach, CA 90809,
U.S.A.

These last two clubs are located in the USA but act as international clubs too. HPX (The Handheld Programming Exchange) has taken over many of the activities of the club CHHU which has closed down. At the time of writing (June 1988) the US PPC club exists but has not been in contact with most members since May of 1987.

NOTES

You may want to put new club addresses here.

APPENDIX B - PROBLEMS

Only a perfect product works perfectly. In our technological society we rarely meet such a thing. The next best thing is a good product, one which has few faults, and whose faults are known so they can be worked around. By this standard the HP-28 is a good product because it has few faults, and it becomes a better product if users know what those faults are and how to avoid them. That is the aim of this appendix - to describe known faults and problems so users can avoid them and get the best from their HP-28s.

The HP-18, HP-19 and HP-28 battery compartment holds two batteries touching end-to-end. The battery compartment is noticeably wider than the batteries - this means that if a battery corrodes and swells then it can still be removed. It also means that if the calculator is moved around a lot then the tip of one battery rubs against the base of the other, and this can lead to oxidation and poor conductivity. That in turn can lead to insufficient power being delivered to the calculator, so that on a few calculators the display fades, the keyboard stops responding, or even Memory Lost occurs. This only happens on a few calculators, but it is better to be safe than sorry. There are three ways to avoid such problems. The first is to remove the batteries about once a week and clean the ends with a pencil eraser. At the same time this lets you check if the batteries are swelling or leaking. The second is to use batteries whose design minimizes this problem. Kodak and Panasonic batteries are recommended by HP, the Kodak batteries are best because they have gold-plated tips (at least those sold in the U.S. do) which should reduce oxidation, and because they are a little longer than other makes, so the contact between them is better. The third way is to increase the strength of the spring in the battery compartment so the batteries are pushed harder against each other. This has been now been done by Hewlett-Packard.

Most people discover a few HP-28 actions which confuse them or appear to be contrary to what they would expect. Some people, for example, are unhappy when they find that UNDO is not self-cancelling; if you press UNDO then the present stack is replaced by the stack as it was before it was most recently changed - but pressing UNDO at once a second time does not bring back the stack as it was before UNDO was pressed the first time. This means you cannot recover the stack if you press UNDO by mistake instead of LAST. My personal example is forgetting to clear the display after drawing a plot. Typically I press SHIFT PLOT to plot another function, and get just a warning tone. Then I remember that I should have pressed ATTN to clear the display, so I press ATTN. The whole display goes blank, and the HP-28 refuses to respond to the keyboard! After about half a minute of desperate worrying and keyboard-prodding, I press ATTN again, and the HP-28 turns on as if there was nothing wrong. Why should this happen? Pressing SHIFT and any other key, except the menu row, SHIFT, or ATTN, sounds the warning tone, but leaves SHIFT activated, so by pressing ATTN next, I simply turn the HP-28 off! This action is unexpected, but it is not a mistake or a fault - it can be described as an unpleasant surprise, but not as a "bug".

"Bug" is the term used to describe some action which is clearly wrong and has to be avoided. Some actions are half way between being an unpleasant surprise and a real bug. For example Frank Wales described the following to me. Turn on a version 1BB HP-28C and keep the ON key pressed down for a moment before lifting your finger from it. Now press SHIFT; there is a 50% chance that the HP-28C will turn off at once. If it does not, then press ON again to turn the HP-28C off, then press ON to turn it on and keep the ON key down a moment again. Press SHIFT again and this time the HP-28C will turn off. This is clearly wrong, pressing SHIFT on its own should not turn the HP-28 off! What happens is that keeping your finger down on the ON key stores a keystroke in the key buffer, and when SHIFT is pressed then the HP-28 "thinks" that you have pressed SHIFT ON, so it turns off. The design team accepted that this was a problem, and it has been corrected on newer versions of the HP-28. On the other hand this does not cause the HP-28Cs affected to give any incorrect results, to write incorrect programs, or to stop working properly.

The following is a list of known real bugs which can cause problems such as those just described. My thanks go to Tony Collinson and other people at HP who warned me of many of them, and to Brian Walsh who listed a selection of bugs in V1N2 and V1N3 of the HPX Exchange. These bugs have all been reported on version 1BB HP-28Cs, but many have been removed on later versions - see the note below and Appendix E.

1. Using the Solver with programs which do not add a result to the stack (and thus increase the stack depth) can put a System Object on the stack. Do not use such equations or programs with the Solver, and if you do get a System Object from the Solver then do a System Halt to clear the stack.

2. Trying to delete an empty row with SHIFT INS while editing a command line containing one or more lines can lead to strange results on the line or even Memory Lost. If you do this press ATTN or ENTER to end editing.

3. Dividing a 64 bit binary integer with its leading bit set can give wrong results. Do not divide anything into binary numbers larger than $2^{63} - 1$.

4. Binary integers with different word sizes are considered not equal even if they contain equal numbers. The word size of a binary integer is 64 bits unless it has been stored with a different word size in effect or is the result of a calculation with a different word size in effect. Try #1 DUP 50 STWS 'A' STO 'A ENTER == and the result is 0 even though both objects have the value #1. The #1 on the stack is still 64 bits long, but the value stored in 'A' is 50 bits long. To avoid this problem always make sure the two numbers being compared have the same word size, you can do this by adding #0 to both of them before doing the test, and never compare a number on the stack with one which stored in a variable.

5. If flags 57 or 58 are set then the Solver might give an underflow or an overflow error while it is iterating towards a solution. Do not use SOLV with these flags set.

6. The Solver can also give incorrect "Sign Reversal" messages. Check points near the one at which you get this message and if you do not believe it then try starting at a different value, or rewriting the equation.

7. Do not define your own units that are multiples of degrees Fahrenheit or Celsius. These will give the wrong results, apparently because degrees involve both additive and multiplicative constants.

8. The unit "yr" has been defined as a calendar year of 365 days instead of a solar year of (approximately) 365.242 days. The light year "lyr" is defined in terms of this too. The same numbers are given in the Reference Manual too.

9. RND does not work correctly in FIX mode. Try 0 FIX .7 RND and you get 0. instead of 1. unless you have flag 51 or 52 set! If you want to use RND in FIX mode then set one or both of the flags 51 or 52. If you do not want to do so (you are using a battery-powered printer and you want to have audible error messages) then do ->STR STR-> to round the number. This can demonstrate another problem, do 0 FIX, then MAXR ->NUM and you see 1.E500. Now ->STR gives "1.E500", but then STR-> gives "Syntax Error".

10. String comparisons do not work properly if the strings have the same first letter. For example "AA" "AB" < gives 0.

11. EDIT (and VISIT) can give unexpected results if you try to insert CHS or EEX into a number that already exists in the command line. If necessary, delete the old number and put in the new one, or use the - sign and the letter E instead of CHS and EEX when editing numbers in programs.

12. Incorrect use of the derivative function has been reported to cause memory corruption. Do not give incorrect parameters to this function.

13. Merge left in the Algebra FORM menu can give wrong results with the divide sign.

14. Rounding of numbers in CMPLX and MATRIX arithmetic is sometimes inaccurate (results are not exactly the same as they would have been for the same operation using real numbers). You can usually check the accuracy of results by using the inverse function.

15. Plotter tick marks are placed relative to the screen, not relative to the plot origin when the origin is not on the screen. This means that you may not get correct scale marks if you try to make a large plot by printing several plots with PRLCD and putting them next to one another.

16. The HP-28 has a "key buffer" which stores up to 15 keystrokes if you press keys one after another faster than the HP-28 can deal with them. The keystrokes are then taken from this key buffer and interpreted. Thus if you are repeatedly carrying out an operation by pressing a menu key then that key might be stored one or more times in the key buffer. Now, if the HP-28C runs out of memory while some of these keystrokes are in the buffer then it goes into the Out of Memory procedure and puts up the YES and NO menu keys. If any keystrokes on these keys are still left in the key buffer, then they are interpreted as YES or NO, so you may find that variables which you are using get deleted without any warning. If these are running programs then this might lead to a Memory Lost. You should therefore avoid pressing the two leftmost menu keys repeatedly and quickly if there is any chance that this will lead to Out of Memory.

17. The Solver does not always clear an internal flag while going from one iteration to the next. To demonstrate this, do a Memory Lost, then 0   1/X. This gives "Infinite Result" and sets the flag.

DROP the 0 and STO << A DROP 1 >> as the Solver equation. Try to solve for A without an initial guess. This will lead to a System Halt. The bug is not commonly encountered, and if it does come up then the System Halt will tell you something has happened.

18. If the Solver gets a "Non-real Result" error then it can store a "System Object" as the value of the variable being solved for.

19. Some special characters are incorrectly shown in the menu line. For example the vertical bar (character number 124 "|") is shown as "Z". Try the following: 1 "N" 124 CHR + STR-> STO and you will see a new variable whose name is displayed in the menu as NZ instead of N|. This is the most extreme example, but few people are likely to use | in a variable name. Other characters affected are ~ and the multiplication and division signs x and ÷. The proportionality sign (character 140) shows up in a most unusual shape, and "&" shows up as "e". This last might not be a mistake, since "&" is actually a contraction of "et" and is sometimes written that way, but it is confusing.

20. When you edit programs containing clauses which end with a matrix you might find a phantom } displayed in the program. As an example type:

<< IF 1 THEN 1 [1]   ENTER

This should produce the program << IF 1 THEN 1 [1] END >> but instead you will see:

<< IF 1 THEN 1 [1] } END >>

If you press EVAL then you will see that 1 and [1] have been pushed onto the stack but the } has not shown up. This means that it is a "phantom }" - the text string you have typed in was correctly "compiled" into the first program; then the program was "decompiled" again so it could be displayed. The decompiler has become confused by the end of the matrix followed at once by the end of the THEN clause, and has lost count of things that have ended. The end of a list is not stored as a special object, so an unmatched spare end is interpreted as a list end, and the decompiler displays that. The error can occur in the THEN or ELSE clause of an IF or an IFERR, and in the REPEAT clause of a WHILE...REPEAT program structure, if any of these clauses ends with a matrix which has at least one other object before it. Since this is a "phantom }" it does not affect the programs, unless you try to edit them; if you press ENTER after EDIT or VISIT then the unwanted } becomes a real } in the text string which is the decompiled program, and is treated as a syntax error when you finish editing. Worse still, if you put a list into the program while editing it, and accidentally leave out the } of this list then the phantom } will become the end of the list, probably in quite the wrong place! If you edit a program containing one or more such phantom curly brackets you should therefore delete them before doing anything else.

* * *

The following are on the border between "unexpected actions" and bugs, but I thought I'd put them here anyway!

21. If you VISIT a variable and edit it so that there is nothing left in the command line then it is not clear what the HP-28 should put in that variable when you press ENTER. What the HP-28 actually does put in is the object in level 1! (If you are not aware of this then you will not know what has happened to what was in level 1.) This is a natural result of the way EDIT works - VISIT uses EDIT - so HP will probably not consider this to be a bug - but really you should get an error message telling you that you have tried to store a null string in a variable. The problem becomes more serious if you do this while VISITing the stack; try the following:

i. Clear the stack and press 5 ENTER 4 ENTER 3 ENTER 2 ENTER 1 ENTER.

ii. Edit level 3 by pressing 3 VISIT, and the SPACE key to remove the 3.

iii. Press ENTER to finish editing level 3.   As there is only a blank space left there, the HP-28 takes the value from level 1 so as to put it in level 3.   It uses the new value to replace level 3 (which you were editing), but the 1 has been taken out of level 1, so the stack has dropped and it is the 4 which has dropped to level 3 that is replaced by the 1, while the 3 which you were editing remains in level 2.

The upshot of this operation is that the stack contents have quite unexpectedly changed from   5,4,3,2,1   to   5,1,3,2.   The moral is, don't try to edit variables or stack objects so they will consist only of blanks.

22.   NEWLINE sometimes behaves oddly.   It is actually a character like any other, such as "A" or "7" or "$" and is often treated as such, but because its ASCII code (10 decimal) is outside the normal range it is displayed as a square box (#). For example if you type ", A, NEWLINE, B, ENTER then you will see the text string "A#B".   If you try to EDIT or VISIT this string then the square box vanishes and B appears correctly on a new line.   The backarrow key cannot be used to delete a NEWLINE character, but you can move the cursor to the right of the A on the upper line and press DEL to remove it.   If you do this, then press NEWLINE again, a new line will be put between the A and the B - NEWLINE is always inserted, it never replaces the current character, so the B is not replaced even though the HP-28 is in replace mode.   If you are entering a program or a set of numbers then NEWLINE is treated as a separator, like SPACE or the comma (point if you use comma as a radix mark) and is replaced by a space (or the non-radix mark in complex numbers) when you press ENTER.

That brings me to the "bug".   Type in this program, exactly as below:

<< "WHAT IS X? 1 DISP

and press ENTER.   You will see that the " which should have been after X? is missing, so the HP-28 thoughtfully put it in for you, at the end of the program.   EDIT the program, replace the space after

X? with ", then press ENTER. The text string "WHAT IS X?" will now show up correctly, but the unmatched " at the end of the program will swallow up the NEWLINE (put there by the decompiler) and >> which were after it, so the program will now have an unwanted " >>" at the end!   I am sure that HP will argue this is your own fault, but I am inclined to treat it as a bug, as is Bruce Bailey who first told me of it. Either way, be careful with NEWLINEs!

A few other things should be avoided. Remember that self-reference can lead to an infinite loop. Any program that refers to itself can call itself repeatedly, and unless there is a clear way to end the recursion it will eventually fill up the memory. Attempting to turn a text string into a name will hang up the HP-28 if that name already exists. Say you want to create a variable with the name "N!". You have to create this name as a text string first ("N" 33 CHR +), then you can use STR-> to convert the text string into a name. If the name exists already then the HP-28 goes into an infinite loop trying to evaluate the name and coming back with the name itself again. Use System Halt to get out of such infinite loops.

Notes for users of the HP-28S and newer HP-28Cs.
The numbered bugs above, except 12, 13, 19, 20, 21 and 22 are corrected in version 1CC of the HP-28C and in the HP-28S (see Appendix E for more details of these new models). Bugs 12 and 13 may have been reported incorrectly, and the bugs from 19 up are less likely to cause trouble. Minor improvements have been made as well, for example the odd action of the ON key described at the beginning of this appendix has been dealt with.

Some changes in the HP-28S might cause problems, especially to HP-28C users who get an HP-28S. In Alpha Entry mode commands such as + and - are entered with spaces automatically put before and after them; this prevents some syntax errors, but can be very confusing in the case of the -> character. For example, if you type the three characters B -> R then you do not get the command B->R, instead you get the names B and R separated by the local variable creation command ->. When you type in such a program and press ENTER, the HP-28S says there is a SYNTAX ERROR but does not identify -> as the source of the error. To avoid this, press alpha once before and twice after ->, so there will be no spaces around it, or delete unwanted spaces you may find before and after an ->. If you have moved from an HP-28C to an HP-28S look out for problems such as this due to changes in the HP-28S; a list of differences is given in Appendix E.

NOTES

You may want to make notes of other problems here.

APPENDIX C – THE STRUCTURE OF OBJECTS AND PROGRAMS

Everything the HP-28 does is done, at the lowest level, by machine language instructions. Collections of machine language instructions make up machine language subprograms. If need be, a machine language subprogram can use another machine language subprogram but this is still all machine language. At the next level up, higher-level subprograms use these lowest-level subprograms. These higher-level subprograms are written in RPL and they call the machine language subprograms simply by using the address at which each machine language subprogram begins. Just as machine language subprograms can use other machine language subprograms, so RPL subprograms can use ("call") other RPL subprograms. An RPL subprogram is therefore made up of a string of addresses, each address being the address of another subprogram. All this has been shown in the main text, including schematic diagrams in point 4.1. An RPL program written by a user follows the same rules, but is stored in RAM and uses only those RPL subprograms which have names and can be included in programs - these subprograms are called "commands" and they are listed in the Operation Index in the HP-28 Reference Manual. The structure of a user-written program includes commands to define the program, the << and >> commands, and commands at the end of the program, the whole layout was shown at the end of point 3.10.

Programs can include data objects in them. For example the program

<< 17.5 DUP >>

contains the command DUP (stored as address #177F1 on a version 1BB HP-28C) and the data object 17.5 which is a real number. This is made up of a command (address #02933) followed by the real number itself. The command is the address of a subprogram which specifies that the next 16 nybbles contain a real number which is to be put on the stack, and that they are not to be treated as a command. All objects are stored in this way - the address of a subprogram which defines the data, and the data value itself. The defining subprogram is called a "prolog", so objects are stored as a prolog address followed by data. The following shows how an object would be held within a program:

Previous program step

Low address

Address of prolog
D A T A

High address

Next program step

If the object is one with a variable length, such as a text string, or a binary integer (whose length depends on the wordsize), then the length is stored in the first five nybbles of the data. The prolog alone, or the prolog in combination with the length field, defines the total length of the object. In a running program, the pointer D0 has to be moved forward by this length so that it will point to the next command after the object.

Objects do not have to be stored within a program. They can be put on the stack, or stored in a "global" variable or in a local variable. In such cases the object's structure is still the same (except that binary numbers are stored in variables with as many nybbles are required by their word size, whereas at other times they are stored in a field of 64 bits even if the current word size is smaller) but what is stored before or after the object is usually no longer a program step. Objects can also be stored in other objects ("composite" objects). For example an array of real numbers is made up of individual real numbers, or a list is made up of other objects. In the first case, all the objects within an array of real numbers are the same, so the array needs only one prolog, which says "this is an array of real numbers", and the prolog is followed by the array dimensions and then the data making up all the numbers. In the second case, the list prolog can only say "this is a list", but the objects can be of various types, so each object must be stored with its own prolog. The objects in a list do not therefore need to be stored within the list, the list can contain just the address of an object, and the object itself can be stored somewhere else, even within another list. If you want further details, you can find descriptions and diagrams in the August 1987 HP Journal, mentioned in Appendix A and elsewhere in this book.

As was described in point 3.11, RPL allows for more object types than are described in the Reference Manual. Not all objects defined within RPL can actually be handled by the version of RPL that is provided in the HP-28; objects which can be handled by the HP-28 are stored as described above and can be created by the methods described in Chapters 3 and 4. These methods allow you to create non-normalized versions of objects which are recognized by the user interface, and to create objects which are not recognized correctly by the user interface (decompiler), but which are dealt with correctly by programs. The addresses of the prologs of these objects are given below. Objects whose length cannot be easily defined, such as programs or lists, end with a special command 09F20 which acts as an end-of-object definition.

The single-digit real numbers 0 to 9 and -9 to -1 are stored in programs not as a prolog and data but as 5 nybble commands. This is similar to the action of the FORTH programming language which usually treats the numbers 0, 1 and 2 as "words" not numbers. In the same way, one-character text strings containing the letters "A" to "Z" are also stored as commands, not objects. Knowing this can help you understand programs you are analyzing, but in principle you can think of these special commands as data objects which contain a prolog with no data.

HP-28S owners should know that subdirectories are rather like lists

- a first level subdirectory is stored like other variables in the HOME menu, and variables in the subdirectory are held inside the subdirectory itself, as if it was a list stored in the HOME menu.

More details than this are really beyond the scope of this book - if you want further details then one place where they have been published (by Paul Courbis) is in issue 51 of JPC, the Journal of the Paris Club (address in Appendix A). If you cannot read French you will be happy to know the article has been translated - you may be less happy to know it has been translated so far only into Danish (in Vol. 8, No. 1 of the Danish club journal USER). With any luck an English version will be published soon in one of the English-language club journals. If you want to follow this subject up you really need to be a bit of a polyglot, since a lot more interesting material is being published in the Dutch club journals by Michiel Niemeijer.

Finally here are the addresses used in prologs to define the various types of objects. These addresses are the same in versions 1BB, 1CC and 2BB of the HP-28. My thanks to Bruce Bailey and Graeme Cawsey for help in compiling this list. Objects marked * are not available for normal HP-28 use but some are used internally.

02911	Short Integer *	02AB8	ROM/RAM pair * (used for
02933	Real		HP-28S subdirectories)
02955	Long real *	02ADA	Algebraic
02977	Complex	02C67	RPL Program
0299D	Long complex *	02C96	In-line machine code *
029BF	Byte *	02D12	Name
029E1	Like array, not used *	02D37	Local name
02A0A	Array	02D5C	ROM pointer (identifies a
02A2C	Like array, not used *		single command, as in point
02A4E	String		2.20)
02A70	Binary Integer	02F90	End a composite object
02A96	List		(program, list, etc.)

Note that all arrays are defined by one address; the prolog has information whether the array is a vector or a matrix and real or complex.

There are only two kinds of name - local and "global". This is the reason why variables are recognized as either local and global, even though not all HP-28S variables are truly global, as was mentioned in chapter 5 - variables are just given the same "name-type" as their names.

NOTES

APPENDIX D – INTERNAL LAYOUT
AND USE OF MACHINE LANGUAGE

Chapters 3 and 4 and Appendix C have given many details of how the HP-28 memory is arranged and how machine code is run, but some details and lists are best given all in one place - that place is here!

Overall Memory Layout. HP-28C ROM and RAM are arranged as below, HP-28S users should see the extra notes that follow the layouts.

Address	Contents
#FFFFF	Top of address space
.	
.	This area is unused, but if additional RAM is built
Unused	into an HP-28 then it is configured into this area,
.	beginning at #50000.
.	
.	
#50000	Bottom of free memory space in an HP-28C
#4FFFF	Top of user RAM in an HP-28C
.	
.	This area is used for storage of the user's programs
User RAM	and variables, for local variables and return
.	addresses, and for other objects created by the
.	system, like flags and pointers
.	
#4F000	Bottom of user RAM
.	
Unused	This area is unused. Display RAM could expand into
.	it on future HP-28 models, but it is unlikely that
.	user RAM could.
.	
#407F0	Top of display RAM
.	

Display RAM . . #40000 #3FFFF	Area used for storage of information to control the display, or I/O, the timers, and as scratch; part of it is unusable. Bottom of display RAM Top of ROM

Display
RAM
.

.

#40000   Bottom of display RAM
#3FFFF   Top of ROM
.

.

.

.   This is the area which contains the HP-28 operating

.   system, it is made up of several large "files" each

System of which looks rather like an HP-71B LEX

.   file.   This   ROM kind of layout allows   the

fundamentals of RPL to be kept in one or two files,

.   the   mathematical operations to be stored in separate

files, and   the   user interface to be in separate

.   files again. A modular system such as this allows

.   rapid changes to be made, and new calculators to be

designed using files which   have already   been

.   developed for previous models.

.

#00000   Bottom of ROM and of address space.

A great many details of the layout of RAM and ROM have been worked out and are being published in user club journals (e.g. articles by Paul Courbis in the PPC Paris Journal). There is not room to put all these details in this book, but some have already been given, for example details of how variables are stored at the top of RAM were shown in point 3.9. As control of the display is one of the topics most likely to interest machine code programmers, here is the layout of the HP-28C display RAM.

The display RAM. This is best treated as a collection of 8 nybble objects each of which plays some special role.

Address   Contents and explanation

#40000   Contains FFFFF000 for the "busy" annunciator to be turned on, otherwise contains all zeroes.

#40008   As #40000 but for Alpha annunciator

#40010   Same, battery.

#40018   Same, SHIFT

#40020   Same, RAD (two pi)

#40028   Same, suspended program

#40030   Same, printer

#40038   The above addresses act as "column" drivers for each of the annunciators, this address acts as a "row" driver, so when it is set it inverts the setting of all the annunciators.

#40040 - #40060 Scratch area

#40068   Contains xxxIJNNF where xxx is scratch, I is 0 until the printer is used, then it is 8. This appears to be a flag defining the direction of I/O on the one-bit master display driver I/O line. J is usually F, but becomes E after printing. NN is a cyclic count of turn-ons. It begins at 00, then after OFF/ON becomes 11, then 22, and so on up to FF, then back to 00. The last digit is always F.

#40070   Scratch

#40078 - #402DE   77 eight-nybble numbers each of which contains a description of which pixels are turned on and which are off in a vertical column of the display. These numbers describe columns at the left of the display, controlled by the slave display driver. The first number describes the leftmost column.

#402E0 - #402F8 Contain 00000000 and cannot be changed.

#40300 & #40308 Contains 0008888888000000. Changing this number can destroy control of the display, though changes to the leftmost two nybbles have little effect.

#40310 - #403F0 Contain 00000000 and cannot be changed.

#403F8   Slave display driver timer, used to time 0.49 seconds between lines of output sent to the printer.

#40400 - #405D8 60 eight-nybble numbers used like #40078 - #402DE but for the right hand columns controlled by the master display driver.

#405E0 - #406D8   32 eight-nybble numbers controlling which "logical" rows in the column control numbers (see above) will actually control which "physical" rows. #405E0 is normally 10000000 which means that the bottom row of the display is controlled by the bits at the bottom of each column descriptor. #405E8 is normally 00000008 which means that the top row of the display is controlled by the bits at the top of each column. The eight-nybble numbers alternate between ones describing the lower half of the display, from the bottom up, and numbers describing the top half, from the top down.

#406E0 - #406F8 Contain 00000000 and cannot be changed.

#40700 & #40708 Similar to #40300 & #40308 - used to control the display and dangerous to change.

#40710 - #407F0 Contain 66666666 and cannot be changed.

#407F8   Master display driver timer used to control the system clock and timing operations such as turn-off after the counter has passed 10 minutes.

I am grateful to Graeme Cawsey who set me off on the trail of studying all this. A similar list of addresses in main RAM would take up many pages; many of the addresses are moveable, with the position of objects defined by pointers. A list has been published by Paul Courbis for the HP-28C (see previous Appendix) and he promises a similar list for the HP-28S.

HP-28S RAM and ROM. The layout of RAM and ROM in the HP-28S is a little different. The 32K bytes of RAM lie in the area from #C0000 to #CFFFF. Exactly the same area of RAM can also be addressed between #D0000 and #DFFFF. Why this should be so is an interesting question! It has been suggested that one of the address bits is ignored so that D (1101 binary) and C (1100 binary) cannot be distinguished. In that case though, addresses beginning with E should be indistinguishable from addresses beginning with F, but this clearly not the case, as #FFFFF is not the same as #EFFFF - the former is the top of the display RAM whereas the latter is empty. It may be that the lowest wire of the 32K RAM chip selector in the HP-28S is not connected (a suggestion made to me by Paul Courbis); my pet theory is that the HP-28S was originally designed with two RAM controllers, so each could control a 4K RAM chip, but then one 32K RAM chip was put in instead, and both controllers are connected to it, giving it two possible addresses.

The HP-28S display RAM has also been moved; it is now between #FF800 and #FFFFF. Thus to use the display RAM layout given above, add #BF800 to the HP-28C addresses to get the HP-28S addresses. Most of the contents are the same, though some of the scratch areas have been moved around.

The position of ROM has not changed in the HP-28S but nearly all the code in it has been moved around. Appendix E includes a list of HP-28C version 1BB addresses used in this book, and where they have moved to in the HP-28S (and in version 1CC of the HP-28C).

The Saturn CPU. The CPU (Central Processor Unit, the chip which controls the calculator) used in the HP-28, the HP-18C and other new HP calculators, is a new version of the Saturn CPU previously used in the HP-71B handheld computer. This CPU is a CMOS device, for low power consumption, and runs at 617kHz, though it can run at up to 1MHz, and versions exist that can run much faster than that. (Running the chip really fast can heat it up and use up the batteries too fast for a handheld device which is meant to be portable and to need new batteries only every few months. The CPU in the HP-28S and more recent calculators runs at 1MHz.) Most data transfers are done on a bus which is only four bits wide, so as to reduce the number of connections on the board, and hence the size of the calculator. Details of the original Saturn CPU have been published in the IDS and in HP Journals (see Appendix A). Details are also available in "The Basic HP-71", in the notes from the 1985 Atlanta HP Handheld Conference, in the user club journals PPC Journal (article by John Baker in V12N2 pages 4 to 12), PPC Computer Journal (V2N6), CHHU Chronicle (V1N1 & V2N1) and in issues of the PPC-Paris Journal (JPC) and issue 6 of NUTS, the journal of the Dutch club HP Club Twente. The best place to look for these is a user club library!

In the first edition of this book (a preliminary version dated December 1987) I gave a list of the addresses of commands in the HP-28C version 1BB ROM. This list was useful in studying the HP-28 memory layout - now that such studying has been done, and the layout has changed in the newer versions, the list is less useful, so it is not given in this edition. Instead I give a description of the Saturn CPU and its instructions, since HP have now given permission to publish the details - many thanks to HP.

The Saturn CPU is optimized for arithmetic, on numbers with 12 digit mantissas and 3 digit exponents. Such numbers are stored in 16 nybble registers; one extra nybble for the mantissa sign. Internally the calculators do a lot of their arithmetic on extended precision numbers, with a 15 digit mantissa stored in one register and a 5 nybble exponent stored in a second register. By no means do all operations use a 16 nybble register. For example addresses are only 5 nybbles long, so the Saturn defines "fields" within a 16 nybble register, these will be described later. The CPU has four 16 nybble operating registers, A, B, C and D which are used for most operations and for arithmetic. It has five more 16 nybble registers for temporary storage; R0, R1, R2, R3 and R4. The two data address pointers D0 and D1 are 5 nybbles long each. There is a 5 nybble program counter (PC), an eight level subroutine return stack (RTN), and a 4 nybble status register (ST) holding 16 flags, plus a separate Carry flag (C) set by arithmetic carry operations. There are an input and output register, (IN and OUT; 4 and 3 nybbles long respectively, used to read the keyboard and to send configuration commands and for beeper control) and there is a one nybble long pointer register (P), used when you need to define arbitrary fields within a 16 nybble register. Finally there is a one nybble hardware status register (HST) whose 4 bits store the status flags. On the HP-71B these are: sticky bit (SB, set when a bit is shifted out of the right of a working register), service request (SR), module pulled (MP) and external module missing (XM, set if an instruction jumps to an empty address). On the HP-28 the last two are not used for their original purposes, but may be used for something else. Here is a summary:

WORKING REGISTERS

A, B, C, D
64 bits long each

Used for data handling
and arithmetic, A and C
are also used for data
transfer to and from
memory. C is the CPU
workhorse for nearly
all data transfers and
most arithmetic.

SCRATCH REGISTERS

R0, R1, R2, R3, R4
64 bits long each

Used to hold temporary
copies of the working
registers. The bottom
20 bits of R4 are used
for interrupt handling
so they should not be
used for data storage.

DATA POINTER REGISTERS

D0, D1
20 bits each

Used for pointing to data
to be copied to and from
working registers.

FIELD POINTER REGISTER

P
4 bits

Used for field selection,
see below for details of
field selection.

PROGRAM CONTROL   STATUS FLAGS & I/O

PC and 8 RTN addresses   C (1 bit), ST (16 bits),
   20 bits each   HST (4 bits in order MP,SR,SB,XM)
                IN (16 bits), OUT (12 bits).

Operations which do not use a whole 16 nybble register have to be told which part of a register, or which "field", they are to use. The fields are shown below:

16 Nybble register

15: 14: 13: 12: 11: 10: 9: 8: 7: 6: 5: 4: 3: 2: 1: 0:


```
                              |<------A------->|
      S                       XS|<--B-->|
|<----------------------M---------------------->|<----X---->|
```


A table of Saturn instructions follows.   Each instruction has a name, or "mnemonic", and a numerical representation, which is the actual number used in machine language programs. Instructions which need to select a field are followed by a "modifier" which specifies the field to be operated on by that instruction. In the mnemonics the modifier is a field select (fs) symbol which is the name of the field.   In the numeric instructions the modifier is an actual number - some use a number in the range 0-7, others use a number in the range 8-F. Ones which use the first will be marked (a) in the instruction list, the others will be marked (b). The names, positions, symbols and representations are:

Field name	Nybbles	Field (fs)	Representation (a)	(b)
Nybble pointed to by P		P	0	8
Word from nybble 0 to nybble pointed to by P		WP	1	9
Exponent sign,	nybble 2	XS	2	A

Exponent (including sign),	nybbles 0-2	X	3	B
Sign,	nybble 15	S	4	C
Mantissa,	nybbles 3-14	M	5	D
Byte (or exponent),	nybbles 0-1	B	6	E
Whole register,	nybbles 0-15	W	7	F
Address field	nybbles 0-4	A - always called A		

Note that instructions which use the A field have only one representation, there is no ambiguity because it is clear which instructions refer to an address, for example C(A) means the address field of register C. The numeric values of addresses will be represented by hhhh if they are 4-digit addresses, and by hhhhh if they are five-digit addresses. Some instructions use a modifier which is not a field selector (fs), but a number of digits for the instruction to use - this is written as (d). Instructions which move data do not move 0 nybbles, so when d has a value of 1, it can be stored as 0, and 16 (dec) can be stored as F - you will see what this means when you look at the list of instructions - here it is:

Numeric value	Mnemonic	Modifier	Brief explanation
00	RTNSXM		Return and set module missing bit; any address in a part of memory that contains no ROM or RAM will contain a zero and will therefore be treated as this code.
00	RTNYES		Return if test true; used after tests - if Carry flag was set by the test then return. See end of list for corresponding GOYES.
01	RTN		Return (pop address from return stack to PC)
02	RTNSC		Return, set carry
03	RTNCC		Return, clear carry
04	SETHEX		Set CPU to do its arithmetic in HEX mode
05	SETDEC		Set CPU to do its arithmetic in DEC mode

06	RSTK=C		Push C(A) onto return stack
07	C=RSTK		Pop value from return stack to C(A)
08	CLRST		clear bits 0-11 in ST
09	C=ST		copy ST(0-11) to C(X)
0A	ST=C		copy C(X) to ST(0-11)
0B	CSTEX		exchange C(X) with ST(0-11)
0C	P=P+1		increment P, go from F to 0 and set carry
0D	P=P-1		decrement P, go from 0 to F and set carry
0Ea0	A=A&B	fs	logical A = A AND B, using (a) field select
0Ea1	B=B&C	fs	logical B = B AND C, as above
0Ea2	C=C&A	fs	etc.
0Ea3	D=C&D	fs *	
0Ea4	B=B&A	fs	
0Ea5	C=C&B	fs	
0Ea6	A=A&C	fs	
0Ea7	C=C&D	fs	
0Ea8	A=A!B	fs	logical A = A OR B
0Ea9	B=B!C	fs	
0EaA	C=C!A	fs *	
0EaB	D=C!D	fs *	
0EaC	B=B!A	fs	
0EaD	C=C!B	fs	
0EaE	A=A!C	fs	
0EaF	C=C!D	fs	
0EF0	A=A&B	A	logical A = A AND B, using A fields of both etc.
0EF1	B=B&C	A	
0EF2	C=C&A	A	
0EF3	D=C&D	A *	
0EF4	B=B&A	A	
0EF5	C=C&B	A	
0EF6	A=A&C	A	
0EF7	C=C&D	A	
0EF8	A=A!B	A	
0EF9	B=B!C	A	
0EFA	C=C!A	A *	

0EFB	D=C!D	A *	
0EFC	B=B!A	A	
0EFD	C=C!B	A	
0EFE	A=A!C	A	
0EFF	C=C!D	A	
0F	RTI		return and enable interrupts
100	R0=A		copy A(W) - all 64 bits of A - to R0
101	R1=A		etc.
102	R2=A		
103	R3=A		
104	R4=A		
108	R0=C		
109	R1=C		
10A	R2=C		
10B	R3=C		
10C	R4=C		
110	A=R0		
111	A=R1		
112	A=R2		
113	A=R3		
114	A=R4		
118	C=R0		
119	C=R1		
11A	C=R2		
11B	C=R3		
11C	C=R4		
120	AR0EX		exchange A(W) and R0
121	AR1EX		
122	AR2EX		
123	AR3EX		
124	AR4EX		
128	CR0EX		
129	CR1EX		
12A	CR2EX		
12B	CR3EX		
12C	CR4EX		
130	D0=A		D0=A(A), address field of A to D0

131	D1=A	
132	AD0EX	exchange D0 with A(A)
133	AD1EX	
134	D0=C	
135	D1=C	
136	CD0EX	
137	CD1EX	
138	D0=AS	copy A "short" (0-3) to low 4 nybbles of D0
139	D1=AS	
13A	AD0XS	exchange A and D0 "short" (nybbles 0:3)
13B	AD1XS	
13C	D0=CS	
13D	D1=CS	
13E	CD0XS	
13F	CD1XS	
140	DAT0=A A *	copy A(A) to address pointed to by D0 Warning: the IDS gives the wrong code (146) for this & for the other DAT0=A instructions, see notes below.
141	DAT1=A A	
142	A=DAT0 A	copy from address pointed to by D0 to A(A)
143	A=DAT1 A	
144	DAT0=C A	
145	DAT1=C A	
146	C=DAT0 A	
147	C=DAT1 A	
148	DAT0=A B *	copy A(B) to address pointed to by D0
149	DAT1=A B	
14A	A=DAT0 B	
14B	A=DAT1 B	
14C	DAT0=C B *	
14D	DAT1=C B	
14E	C=DAT0 B	
14F	C=DAT1 B	

150a	DAT0=A	fs *	copy field from A as selected by (a) codes
151a	DAT1=A	fs	
152a	A=DAT0	fs	
153a	A=DAT1	fs	
154a	DAT0=C	fs	
155a	DAT1=C	fs	
156a	C=DAT0	fs	
157a	C=DAT1	fs	
158x	DAT0=A	d *	copy field from A using lowest d(=x+1) digits
159x	DAT1=A	d	
15Ax	A=DAT0	d	
15Bx	A=DAT1	d	
15Cx	DAT0=C	d *	
15Dx	DAT1=C	d	
15Ex	C=DAT0	d	
15Fx	C=DAT1	d	
16x	D0=D0+	n	add n to D0 (n=x+1), set Carry if carries
17x	D1=D1+	n	
18x	D0=D0-	n	
19hh	D0=(2)		copy hh to D0, also called D0=HEX hh
1Ahhhh	D0=(4)		copy hhhh to D0, also called D0=HEX hhhh
1Bhhhhh	D0=(5)		copy hhhhh to D0, also called D0=HEX hhhhh
1Cx	D1=D1-	n	
1Dhh	D1=(2)		
1Ehhhh	D1=(4)		
1Fhhhhh	D1=(5)		
2n	P=	n	copy n to pointer P
3xn...n	LC(m)	n...n	Load C with value n...n , m digits
	LCASC	\A...A\	long, beginning at P position,
	LCHEX	h...h	towards higher nybbles, wrap around if need.This instruction has 3 different names depending on whether

		it is used to load a constant, ASCII or HEX values, but all work the same.
400	RTNC	return if Carry flag set
4hh	GOC	jump relative if Carry, offset hh from nybble of the opcode, hh in two's complement and back-to-front, see next line.
420	NOP3	3 nybble null operation, skips over itself
500	RTNNC	return if carry flag not set
5hh	GONC	jump if no carry, see GOC (4hh) for details
6hhh	GOTO hhh	unconditional 3 nybble relative jump
6300	NOP4	4 nybble NOP
64000	NOP5	5 nybble NOP, the last 0 is just a filler
7hhh	GOSUB	save next address on RTN stack, jump relative
800	OUT=CS	put C(S) in output register(S) (system bus)
801	OUT=C	put C(X) in whole OUT register (system bus)
802	A=IN	copy IN register to A(3:0)
803	C=IN	
804	UNCNFG	unconfigure all chips, & load C(A) into each chip controller's data pointer
805	CONFIG	configure; send C(A) to chip which has daisy chain input high and config flag low
806	C=ID	identify chip; send chip ID of chip with daisy chain input high & config low to C(A)
807	SHUTDN	send bus shutdown command and stop CPU clock
8080	INTON	enable keyboard interrupts
808?	new opcodes	new Saturn opcodes - see notes at end

808F	INTOFF		disable keyboard (except ATTN key)
809	C+P+1		add P+1 to C(A), always done in HEX mode
80A	RESET		send system bus reset command, resets chips
80B	BUSCC		send system bus command "C" - not used on '71
80Cn	C=P	n	copy P into nybble n of C
80Dn	P=C	n	
80E	SREQ?		set SR if any chip on bus requests service; if so, device identifier is latched to C(0)
80Fn	CPEX	n	exchange C(n) with P
810	ASLC		A shift left circular, 1 nybble, sticky bit (SB) not affected
811	BSLC		B shift left circular, as above
812	CSLC		
813	DSLC		
814	ASRC		A shift right circular, SB set if nybble shifted from 0 to F position was non-zero
815	BSRC		
816	CSRC		
817	DSRC		
81C	ASRB		A shift right 1 bit, low bit lost, SB set if it was non-zero, zero put in high bit
81D	BSRB		
81E	CSRB		
81F	DSRB		
821	XM=0		clear XM flag
822	SB=0		clear sticky bit
824	SR=0		clear service request bit
828	MP=0		clear module pulled bit
82?	combine the above		these 4 instructions can be ORed to clear combinations;
82F	CLRHST		82F clears all hard stat flags

831yy	?XM=0		test XM bit, must follow by RTNYES/GOYES (yy) see end of list for GOYES explanation
832yy	?SB=0		test SB bit, must be followed by yy
834yy	?SR=0		
838yy	?MP=0		
84n	ST=0	n	clear bit (flag) n in ST
85n	ST=1	n	set bit n in ST
86nyy	?ST=0	n	test ST bit n, follow with RTNYES/GOYES (yy)
87nyy	?ST=1	n	test ST bit n, again follow with yy
88nyy	?P#	n	test if P not equal to n, yy must follow
89nyy	?P=	n	
8A0yy	?A=B	A	test B(A) equal to A(A), yy must follow
8A1yy	?B=C	A	note that this code can be written
8A2yy	?A=C	A	?C=B A etc.
8A3yy	?C=D	A *	
8A4yy	?A#B	A	test B(A) not equal to A(A)
8A5yy	?B#C	A	
8A6yy	?A#C	A	
8A7yy	?C#D	A	
8A8yy	?A=0	A	test A(A) equal to zero
8A9yy	?B=0	A	
8AAyy	?C=0	A	
8AByy	?D=0	A	
8ACyy	?A#0	A	
8ADyy	?B#0	A	
8AEyy	?C#0	A	
8AFyy	?D#0	A	
8B0yy	?A>B	A	once again, these could be written
8B1yy	?B>C	A	?B<A etc.
8B2yy	?C>A	A	
8B3yy	?D>C	A	
8B4yy	?A<B	A *	
8B5yy	?B<C	A	

8B6yy	?C<A	A
8B7yy	?D<C	A
8B8yy	?A>=B	A
8B9yy	?B>=C	A
8BAyy	?C>=A	A *
8BByy	?D>=C	A
8BCyy	?A<=B	A
8BDyy	?B<=C	A
8BEyy	?C<=A	A
8BFyy	?D<=C	A
8Chhhh	GOLONG hhhh	relative jump, hhhh is two's complement distance to go, relative to 3rd nybble of op
8Dhhhhh	GOVLNG hhhhh	absolute goto address hhhhh
8Ehhhh	GOSUBL hhhh	relative long GOSUB
8Fhhhhh	GOSBVL hhhhh	absolute GOSUB to address hhhhh
9a0yy	?A=B	fs	test A=B at selected field, code (a)
9a1yy	?B=C	fs	etc.
9a2yy	?A=C	fs	
9a3yy	?C=D	fs *	
9a4yy	?A#B	fs	
9a5yy	?B#C	fs	
9a6yy	?A#C	fs	
9a7yy	?C#D	fs	
9a8yy	?A=0	fs	
9a9yy	?B=0	fs	
9aAyy	?C=0	fs	
9aByy	?D=0	fs	
9aCyy	?A#0	fs	
9aDyy	?B#0	fs	
9aEyy	?C#0	fs	
9aFyy	?D#0	fs	
9b0yy	?A>B	fs	test A>B at field selected using code
9b1yy	?B>C	fs	(b) etc.
9b2yy	?C>A	fs	
9b3yy	?D>C	fs	
9b4yy	?A<B	fs *	

9b5yy	?B<C	fs	
9b6yy	?C<A	fs	
9b7yy	?D<C	fs	
9b8yy	?A>=B	fs	
9b9yy	?B>=C	fs	
9bAyy	?C>=A	fs *	
9bByy	?D>=C	fs	
9bCyy	?A<=B	fs	
9bDyy	?B<=C	fs	
9bEyy	?C<=A	fs	
9bFyy	?D<=C	fs	
Aa0	A=A+B	fs	arithmetic add selected fields in A and B, in HEX or DEC mode as selected, result in A, adjust Carry flag
Aa1	B=B+C	fs	etc.
Aa2	C=C+A	fs	
Aa3	D=D+C	fs	
Aa4	A=A+A	fs	effectively a 1 bit shift left
Aa5	B=B+B	fs	
Aa6	C=C+C	fs	
Aa7	D=D+D	fs	
Aa8	B=B+A	fs	
Aa9	C=C+B	fs	
AaA	A=A+C	fs	
AaB	C=C+D	fs	
AaC	A=A-1	fs	decrement A in field selected, adjust Carry
AaD	B=B-1	fs	
AaE	C=C-1	fs	
AaF	D=D-1	fs	
Ab0	A=0	fs	set selected field of A to 0, Carry not adj.
Ab1	B=0	fs	
Ab2	C=0	fs	
Ab3	D=0	fs	
Ab4	A=B	fs	

Ab5	B=C	fs	
Ab6	C=A	fs	
Ab7	D=C	fs	
Ab8	B=A	fs	
Ab9	C=B	fs	
AbA	A=C	fs *	
AbB	C=D	fs	
AbC	ABEX	fs	exchange selected fields of A and B
AbD	BCEX	fs	
AbE	ACEX	fs	
AbF	CDEX	fs	
Ba0	A=A-B	fs	
Ba1	B=B-C	fs	
Ba2	C=C-A	fs	
Ba3	D=D-C	fs	
Ba4	A=A+1	fs	
Ba5	B=B+1	fs	
Ba6	C=C+1	fs	
Ba7	D=D+1	fs	
Ba8	B=B-A	fs	
Ba9	C=C-B	fs	
BaA	A=A-C	fs	
BaB	C=C-D	fs	
BaC	A=B-A	fs	
BaD	B=C-B	fs	
BaE	C=A-C	fs	
BaF	D=C-D	fs *	
Bb0	ASL	fs	shift selected field in A left, SB unaffected
Bb1	BSL	fs	
Bb2	CSL	fs	
Bb3	DSL	fs	
Bb4	ASR	fs	
Bb5	BSR	fs	
Bb6	CSR	fs	
Bb7	DSR	fs	
Bb8	A=-A	fs	2's complement selected field of A if

			in HEX mode, 10's complement in DEC mode, Carry set if field not zero, otherwise Carry cleared.
Bb9	B=-B	fs	
BbA	C=-C	fs	
BbB	D=-D	fs	
BbC	A=-A-1	fs	one's complement selected field, clear Carry
BbD	B=-B-1	fs	
BbE	C=-C-1	fs	
BbF	D=-D-1	fs	
C0	A=A+B	A	arithmetic add address fields in A and B, in HEX or DEC mode as selected, result in A, adjust Carry flag
C1	B=B+C	A	etc.
C2	C=C+A	A	
C3	D=D+C	A	
C4	A=A+A	A	
C5	B=B+B	A	
C6	C=C+C	A	
C7	D=D+D	A	
C8	B=B+A	A	
C9	C=C+B	A	
CA	A=A+C	A	
CB	C=C+D	A	
CC	A=A-1	A	decrement A in address field, adjust Carry
CD	B=B-1	A	
CE	C=C-1	A	
CF	D=D-1	A	
D0	A=0	A	set address field of A to 0, Carry not adj.
D1	B=0	A	
D2	C=0	A	
D3	D=0	A	
D4	A=B	A	
D5	B=C	A	

D6	C=A	A	
D7	D=C	A	
D8	B=A	A	
D9	C=B	A	
DA	A=C	A *	
DB	C=D	A	
DC	ABEX	A	exchange address fields of A and B
DD	BCEX	A	
DE	ACEX	A	
DF	CDEX	A	
E0	A=A-B	A	
E1	B=B-C	A	
E2	C=C-A	A	
E3	D=D-C	A	
E4	A=A+1	A	
E5	B=B+1	A	
E6	C=C+1	A	
E7	D=D+1	A	
E8	B=B-A	A	
E9	C=C-B	A	
EA	A=A-C	A	
EB	C=C-D	A	
EC	A=B-A	A	
ED	B=C-B	A	
EE	C=A-C	A	
EF	D=C-D	A *	
F0	ASL	A	shift A left in address field sticky bit (SB) not affected
F1	BSL	A	
F2	CSL	A	
F3	DSL	A	
F4	ASR	A	A shift right address field, SB adjusted
F5	BSR	A	
F6	CSR	A	
F7	DSR	A	

F8	A=-A	A	2's complement address field of A if in HEX mode, 10's complement in DEC mode, Carry set if field not zero, otherwise Carry cleared.
F9	B=-B	A	
FA	C=-C	A	
FB	D=-D	A	
FC	A=-A-1	A	one's complement address field, clear Carry
FD	B=-B-1	A	
FE	C=-C-1	A	
FF	D=-D-1	A	
yy	GOYES		Tests which expect a RTNYES or GOYES to follow immediately in the next two nybbles treat yy=00 as a RTN if test true, other yy values are a 2's complement GOTO relative to the start position of yy. If test is true Carry is set, otherwise it is cleared.
h...h	CON(m)		An m-nybble long constant, often used in the HP-28 to give the address of an RPL routine.
h...h	REL(m)		An m-nybble long constant which is generated relative to something else, but is stored as an absolute value. For example REL(5) 5 generates a 5-nybble constant which is the address of the instruction 5 nybbles ahead of the position of REL(5) itself.

NOTES:

1. HP has let it be known that the Saturn CPU in the HP-28 has some new operation codes, not described in the HP-71B IDS, but they have not released full details of these new instructions. The design team leader, Dr. Bill Wickes, did say that one instruction is

PC=(A), and I found it possible to deduce that this had to be the instruction 808C, as described in Chapter 4. (It loads into PC the address whose address is in the A field of register A.) The HP Journal for August 1987, page 35, mentioned that the new instructions improve data manipulation and that the interrupt structure has been enhanced. The following list of the new codes was given by HP to Pierre David of the Paris user group; I thank Pierre for passing the codes on to me. The codes are 80810 [RSI - Reset System Interrupt], 808A [?CBIT#1, no further explanation], 808B [?CBIT#0, no explanation], 808C [PC=(A)] and 808E [BUSCD, no explanation]. 80810 apparently re-enables clock interrupts, and 808E is presumably used for interrupt handling too (the name BUSCD is analogous to the instruction BUSCC and must be a new bus control command). 808A and 808B appear not to be used in the HP-28C or the HP-28S, by analogy with other Saturn operations they are probably followed by an "nyy" or a "yy" modifier.

2. When a value is read from RAM into a working register the order of its nybbles is reversed, but it is reversed again when it is written back to RAM, so this is not normally noticed. (The individual bits inside nybbles are not reversed.) Instructions which load data directly into the working registers have to allow for this too, so GOTO addresses are stored back to front in instructions, as are values to be loaded by LCHEX. Relative GOTO and GOSUB instructions store a number which must be added to the address of the beginning of that number to get to the new address. If the leading bit of a relative address is set (but remember the value is stored right to left) then this is a backward jump and the number is in 2's complement.

3. The Carry bit is adjusted by arithmetic calculations and logical tests. When a test is true, Carry is set, otherwise it is cleared, and when an arithmetic operation overflows or borrows then again Carry is set, else it is cleared.

4. Just as ordinary software can have bugs, so the microcode instructions which are built into a CPU can have bugs too! For

example programs in the HP-28 sometimes have SETDEC SETHEX where one SETHEX would do - it may be that SETHEX does not work correctly in the Saturn that is used in the HP-28 and this is a work-around. If a you have a program you are absolutely sure should work, but it does not, then maybe you have found a CPU bug - in that case rewrite your code using different instructions.

5. Mnemonics marked with a * in the list above have incorrect numeric codes given to them in the HP-71B Software IDS Volume I, most but not all have been corrected in the Hardware IDS. If you think you have seen an incorrect mnemonic, remember that some can be written in two ways, for example BAEX is the same as ABEX since they both exchange A and B. Equally ?ST=0 is equivalent to ?ST#1 - but note that A=B is not the same as B=A !

6. There are 8 return levels available for subroutine return addresses, but one of these is used by interrupts, so programs should never have more than 7 pending returns. If you need more than 7 levels you can use C=RSTK to save part of the return stack elsewhere, and then RSTK=C to replace it, or you can use PC=(A) instead of return instructions. Whenever a return is executed the return stack drops and a zero is put on its top. If all 8 levels are dropped then another return moves the Program Counter to address 0 - which is the address of the System Halt instructions.

7. As the HP-28 does not come with an assembler or disassembler I have put the instructions in numeric order so they can be used to disassemble a program from its numeric code. I have included the pseudo-ops CON and REL as they are needed to disassemble HP-28 code, but not the others as they are used by the assembler, not by the CPU. If you need more details than are given here then you need either Volume I of the HP-71B Software IDS to get more details of the Saturn CPU, or you should read a book on assembly language programming to understand the ideas behind it.

NOTICE: This instruction list and these notes are taken from the HP-71B IDS with permission from HP for which I am very grateful.

Hewlett Packard Company and the author do not accept any responsibility direct or consequential for any errors in this list or for the results of any use to which these instructions are put.

NOTES

-201-

APPENDIX E - NEW VERSIONS OF THE HP-28

Late in 1987 version 1BB of the HP-28C was replaced by version 1CC, and early in 1988 the HP-28C was replaced by the HP-28S (version 2BB). Use #A SYSEVAL to check which version you have of the HP-28C or HP-28S. The purpose of this Appendix is to make general comments about new versions, to list the new features of the HP-28S, and to list the SYSEVAL addresses that have been mentioned in this book and have changed from version to version. Appendix B has details of bug corrections in the new models.

The manuals initially provided with version 1CC HP-28Cs are the third edition. They have some minor changes, but the values given for the units "yr" and "lyr" are still the original incorrect ones, even though the calculator has the correct values in it. HP-41 users may be interested to learn that the HP-41 "append" and "angle" signs have been added to newer 82240A printers and are shown in the table of characters in the STRING section of the Reference Manual. The HP-28S manuals are rewritten versions of these HP-28C manuals, with some items moved from one manual to the other, with new material, and with the units corrected.

It is entirely possible that HP will introduce more new versions of the HP-28, perhaps an HP-28S with corrections or improvements, or maybe another new model with Input/Output features to let users copy programs and data to a storage medium, and then read them back to the same HP-28 or to another one. After all, typing 30k bytes into an HP-28S which has suffered a Memory Lost is not a popular pastime among users, even if it is very rarely necessary!

If you have an HP-28 with more memory; either an HP-28C with added memory or an HP-28S then you have to change all the programs which rely on the top of memory being at address #4FFFF. If you add 4k bytes to an HP-28C then the top of memory moves up by 8k nybbles, to #51FFF. If you add 32k then it moves up by 64k nybbles, to #5FFFF. The HP-28S has 32k of user memory, with the top address at #CFFFF, so you should change all addresses beginning with #4FF to addresses beginning with #CFF. To ensure that a variable goes at the top of memory you must put the command HOME at the beginning of any HP-28S program which needs to use a definite address. For example the programs PEEK and POKE should both have the command HOME added at the beginning, and #4FF in both programs should be replaced with #CFF in all three places where it occurs. If you find that you have a new version of the HP-28, you must first find the top of memory by using SYSEVAL with various addresses and finding which ones contain something and which do not - those that do not give a "blink" and clear the screen and stack.

New and changed features of the HP-28S. The HP-28S is a major improvement on the HP-28C. It has more memory, runs faster, and provides sub-directories. As it is still an HP-28 it runs programs written for the HP-28C. Its extra features include new operations, new menus, new commands, and the new unit c (speed of light). Here is a full list of the new and changed features of the HP-28S, put together using my own observations, information from Tony Collinson of HP UK, and Brian Walsh's notes in V1N4 of the US journal HPX Exchange - these came in part from Jake Schwartz: my thanks to all these people. I shall abbreviate HP-28C and 28S to C and S.

1. Hardware changes - There are 32k bytes of RAM in the S, compared to 2k in the C. About 32,400 of these are available to the user, as against 1,700 on the C - 19 times more user memory! The CPU clock runs at 1MHz instead of 640kHz - an increase of 56% - very noticeable during plotting and digitising. The electronics have been redesigned, with most parts on one IC, and the 32k RAM is provided by a standard commercial chip. Thus adding more memory is difficult, if not impossible. A new error message, "Power Lost" is used to show that the electronics have detected a low power condition, usually caused by flat batteries, but that the power loss was not bad enough to cause a Memory Lost. When you see "Power Lost" you will find that the display and the stack have been cleared, but variables have not. You should check if any variables have been altered. Some HP-28Ss have the battery compartment lined with foam rubber to prevent the sideways motion of the batteries

described at the beginning of Appendix B. This should certainly reduce the chances of Power Lost or Memory Lost, but you must shake the HP-28S fairly hard to get the batteries out when you want to change them.

2. COMA mode - during the redesigning of the electronics a very low power mode was added. If you press ON, backarrow, and ENTER at the same time then the S turns off, loses the contents of the stack and display, and stops running the clock (values in variables are NOT lost). Mark Cracknell points out that this mode is probably for use when the S is packed; the batteries are packed in the calculator and this mode lets them last longer while it lies in a shop. You can use this mode to preserve the batteries if your S will be unused for a long time.

3. The display has non-glare glass; so reflections from overhead lights are less bother.

4. The manuals have been rewritten, as I have already mentioned. They are printed on a whiter paper, in darker ink, so they are easier to read. An index has been added to the Reference Manual. The "Getting Started" Manual of the HP-28C is now much thicker and is called the "Owner's Manual."

5. Labels printed above keys which select menus are now on light grey rectangles - this increases the legibility of the labels. All the red labels are in smaller letters. Some menus have been moved to different keys, to make room for the new MEMORY and CUSTOM menu keys, only the P key has no shifted function. The spelling of the names of some menus has been changed, for example the use of smaller letters has allowed CMPLX to be rewritten as COMPLX.

6. The USER menu can include variables which are subdirectories (or submenus). Subdirectories can contain lower subdirectories; objects in higher directories are accessible to their subdirectories. USER now contains only variables created by the user; a separate MEMORY menu contains the old commands ORDER, CLUSR, and MEM, plus new

commands CRDIR (create a new USER subdirectory), HOME (reset USER directory from any subdirectory to the main, or home, directory), PATH (make a list of all menus on the path from the current subdirectory to the HOME directory), MENU (create a custom menu), and VARS (create a list with the names of all the variables in the current directory). These features let you put a set of related variables in one subdirectory to avoid confusing them with other variables; CUSTOM menus let you combine built-in commands with your own variables in one menu, and you can create custom menus which prompt for input like the SOLVER menu. CLUSR clears objects only in the current directory and you can delete a subdirectory only after deleting all the variables in it. Two new error messages "Non-Empty Directory" and "Directory Not Allowed" are used to indicate errors. MEM now returns available memory to the nearest half byte, or nybble.

7. The MENU command can also be used with a number to select a built-in menu; I described a way to do the same thing on a C using SYSEVAL in point 3.11.

8. SOLVER menu labels and custom input labels created by MENU are displayed in black on a white background to distinguish them from ordinary menu labels. Display menus which toggle functions such as LAST now show a small rectangle by the selected mode, instead of providing keys such as [-LAST] and [+LAST].

9. SHIFT ALPHA now toggles the action of keyboard menu keys; press SHIFT ALPHA once and you will not need to press SHIFT before pressing a key to select a menu such as COMPLX. Instead of this you will have to press SHIFT C to get the letter C. If you press SHIFT ALPHA a second time then the normal use of SHIFT will be restored. There is no Alpha Lock key. ALPHA toggles three ways between alpha entry mode, algebraic entry mode, and immediate entry mode. See next point for one use of this.

10. The one-character operators + - * / ^ -> < > <= >= % PI Integral, Differential, and Not Equal are entered with spaces

before and after them during program entry. This means they do not accidentally get mistaken for part of a name; to include one of them in a variable name or a command name you must press ALPHA to leave alpha entry mode, press the key, then press ALPHA two more times to get back to alpha entry mode.

11. Some conversion constants have been changed - a radian is now 1/(2PI) and a steradian has the value 1/(4PI) - the C used 1 for both. Photometric units defined in terms of steradians (Lumen, Lux, Phot, Footcandle) have been changed accordingly. The speed of light (c) has been added as a new conversion constant, and the year and light year have been corrected, as they were in version 1CC of the HP-28C - the year is now a solar year of 365.242 (approx.) days instead of a calendar year of 365 days. The CATALOG and UNITS menus no longer have a SCAN key - the NEXT and PREV soft keys do the same job if you keep them down.

12. Binary integers are displayed with 'b', 'o', 'd' or 'h' after the value to show their base. You can input binary integers in the current base by just putting a # before them, or in any of these bases by including one of the appropriate letters after it as well.

13. GETI and PUTI set flag 46 if they cause their index to wrap round, otherwise they clear it. GET, PUT, GETI and PUTI can use an integer, a real number, or a list for the index of an array or a list. Commands, such as GETI, PUTI or integration, which can accept a list of real numbers as an argument on the C will also accept programs or symbolic values in the list on the S. This is because list elements that return numeric values are automatically evaluated when a list is used explicitly as an argument. (The PPAR list used by plotting commands will not work with symbols instead of numbers though.)

14. POS can find the position of an object in a list, and + can be used to add two lists together (as on the C) or to add an object to a list.

15. The algebraic expression A(I) can return the Ith element of an array or list A, and A(I,J) works on two dimensional arrays too. I and J can be real numbers, integers, or objects which evaluate to one of these. This allows array elements (and list elements of the right types) to be used in algebraic expressions.

16. CROSS accepts 2-element vectors and treats them as if they were 3-element vectors with the third element set to zero. (This is an extension of the way real numbers are treated as complex numbers with the imaginary part set to zero.) RND works on complex numbers and on arrays. COMBination and PERMutation functions have been added to the STAT menu.

17. User defined functions (UDFs) can be defined using a program, not just an algebraic expression. This gives you much more power in defining new functions, since they can be expressed as algorithms, not just as formulae.

18. Two new functions in the STRING menu, LCD-> and ->LCD let you save the display in a 548-byte character string and restore the display from that string. These strings can be inverted (inverse video) with NOT, and combined with AND, OR and XOR. (Other strings can also be used with ->LCD and with AND, OR, XOR - this can be exploited to give interesting displays and to encrypt text strings.) During interactive plotting you can copy the display to a string in the stack by pressing the DEL key. You can also send a copy of the display to the printer at any time by pressing ON and L at the same time. The new DGTIZ command allows moving of the cursor, digitising, and saving of the display in a string as is allowed by DRAW during interactive plotting. You can press the Cursor key (next to SHIFT) at these times to see the coordinates of the cursor, shown in line 4. *W and *H have been changed so the position of the central pixel stays the same when the scale is changed. Mathematical errors and exceptions are ignored during plotting, so for example a function which goes to infinity at the origin can be plotted.

19. Programs are displayed and printed with indentations to show structures such as FOR/NEXT clearly. Flag 47 Set selects double-space printing, something many users wanted. PRUSR prints the names of variables in the current directory, PRVAR can be given a list of the names of variables to print. Arrays are printed with the name and dimensions first, then each element on a separate line. When a program or list is printed any numbers in it are printed in STD format and binary integers are printed in 64 bit word size.

20. On the C inverting a singular matrix was always done by perturbing the matrix, giving an approximate solution. The S does this only if flag 59 (infinite result action flag) is clear, otherwise an INV error is signalled and flag 64 (infinite result indicator flag) is set.

21. Error messages include the name of the command which caused the error, for example using DROP in a program when the stack is empty will display a message which includes "DROP Error:" - this helps in debugging programs.

22. Bug fixes: equal binary integers are shown as equal even if their wordsizes differ. The key buffer is NOT cleared when the solver starts - this means a key can be pressed immediately after starting the solver to view its progress. STOsigma will now accept any object type, like STEQ which does this on the C and the S - this might be considered to be a help, or a new bug.

23. The low memory code has been changed - if the command line is so long that it causes a low memory warning it is first saved in the command stack. At Out of Memory an extra option allows clearing of the CUSTOM menu, the HOME menu becomes current, each object's type is displayed, a subdirectory is deleted only if empty, otherwise the objects in it are offered for deletion, and Out of Memory ends if clearing the subdirectory frees enough room. Purging UNDO, LAST or COMMAND does not disable these modes.

24. Clearly the internal code has been extensively rewritten;

SYSEVAL values are changed - see the list which follows. #109Fh tests a new "low battery?" flag, returning a 1 to the stack if there is a low battery condition, or a 0 otherwise.

25. Finally, the self-tests and system operations have been expanded. If OK, the tests end with OK 28S-E   (E for English, the HP-27S displays E too, but European HP-17Bs show I for International). A short keyboard test has been added to the single step self-test; a full keyboard test is provided by pressing ON and NEXT. Pressing ON and DEL at the same time does something which is called "Cancel System Operation" in the S Owner's Manual but is not explained. The C manual is more forthcoming - it calls this Cancel Reset and explains that a System Halt (ON UP) or a Memory Reset can be cancelled, if you change your mind, by keeping ON pressed down, releasing the other keys, pressing and releasing DEL, and finally releasing ON. The same method can be used to cancel the effect of ATTN - if you press ON during a program or a plot operation then you can cancel the ATTN by keeping ON down and pressing DEL, then releasing both.

The rest of this Appendix is a list of SYSEVAL addresses which were given in this book and which may have changed in the new models, or may change in a future model. A column has been left to fill in details of a new model for yourself if you have one. All the addresses are in hexadecimal. If you do not want to examine the whole list here are the most important points. On version 1CC of the HP-28C you will find the system clock at address #1266 (my thanks to Tony Collinson and Kim Holm for divulging this information). On the HP-28S version 2BB the clock is at #11CA. Most other SYSEVAL addresses given in this book will have changed too, but PEEK will still work (see above for changes required by the HP-28S), so you can find new addresses with a little perseverance. For example you can find that the version number and copyright notice begin at address #3FF9B in the HP-28C version 1CC. (Oddly enough, the copyright notice still has 1986 as its date, although the version 1CC code was completed in March 1987.)

SYSEVAL addresses on new versions. The addresses given in the text of this book for use with SYSEVAL are for the original version 1BB HP-28C.   Here is a list of those addresses again, with the corresponding addresses for the newer versions.   In some cases the discovery of a useful SYSEVAL address was purely fortuitous - some of these addresses still exist on version 1CC but few exist on the 2BB.   This is because version 2BB is largely rewritten - to the extent that versions 1BB and 1CC had their code divided up into 10 recognizable separate chunks whereas 2BB has only 9 such pieces. Where I have been unable to identify a corresponding address for the newer models I have tried to give suggestions on alternative ways to get the same result.

Point Number	Purpose of SYSEVAL Operation and comments on it	1BB address	1CC address	2BB address	Future model?
3.1	Version no. (should never change)	#A	#A	#A	#A
3.2	System clock	#123E	#1266	#11CA	
3.3	Set SHIFT	#9C96	#9C61	#1F8A7	
3.3	Cancel SHIFT	#9CA3	#9C6E	#1F8B4	
3.4	50 extra bytes I have not found an address to do this on the 1CC; instead use #11CB to force an "Out of Memory" and then delete unwanted values.	#11AA	see note	not needed	
3.6	Generalized STO On the HP-28S use the programs in point 3.10 to create "Non- Normalized names" and store variables with those names.	#3FBA7	#3FCC8	see note	
	Definition address for a real number. In fact ALL	#2933	#2933	#2933	

the addresses that define objects
are the same on all three models.

3.6   Generalized ->STR   #2DF0B   #2DFCA   see note
Once again HP-28S users cannot
do this but will be able to do
similar things after point 3.10

3.7   UNDO   #329BE   #32AB3   #3E34A

3.7   COMMAND   #9476   #94ED   #20807
This needs 2 SYSEVALs on   #32311   #3248E   #3DD23
versions 1BB and 1CC, but 3 on   #1892B
the 2BB. The 2BB version does not
turn on alpha mode (as COMMAND normally does on the 2BB),
so as to let the user repeat COMMAND in a program.

3.7   +CMD Note that all these give   #7786   #7788   #184A7
-CMD an error message unless   #77A8   #77AA   #184C9
the stack contains at
least one object.

+UND   #F412   #F428   #21E5C (see
-UND   #F44E   #F464   #21E5C no

Note: the HP-28S address toggles UNDO on and off in turn. To
set UNDO without knowing its present state use the subprogram:

<< IFERR #3E34A SYSEVAL THEN #21E5C SYSEVAL END >>

If UNDO is already set then this will UNDO the present stack,
so use this subprogram at the very beginning of any program
that needs to have the UNDO option set.

3.8   BIP   #30B7   #30B7   see note

There is no exact equivalent on the HP-28S, you can use error

4 as below to generate the unused (on the HP-28S) error number 4, but there is no simple way to create other error numbers.

Error #1	#3327	#3327	#3939
Error #2 (not used on HP-28S)	#3333	#3333	#3945
Error #3	#333F	#333F	#3951
Error #4 (not used on HP-28S)	#334B	#334B	#395D

3.9 Throughout this point, and following ones, note that the define a real number, are the same on all three HP-28 versions. Note also that any programs which use a position relative to the top of memory must use the top of memory in your particular HP-28. For example the top of memory on an HP-28S is #CFFFF so the position of the Non-Normalized number is #CFFFF - 20 instead of #4FFFF - 20. As there is no "BIP" address on the HP-28S you will not be able to use your Non-Normalized numbers to get strange error numbers, and as there is no generalized STO you will have to wait till the next point to find how to create "customized" names for variables. WARNING: on the HP-28S any program which stores something at the top of memory must do so from the HOME menu, otherwise the variable will be at the top of the current directory but not necessarily at the top of RAM.

3.10 The method described here to create Non-Normalized names, such as names with algebraic signs in them, is the only method available to HP-28S users (unless someone finds another alternative to Ianization). Once again you have to use the right address for the top of memory in your particular HP-28, for example on an HP-28S replace 327680 with 851968 (the decimal equivalent of #D0000) in the program NNC.

3.10 SST	#105BC	#105F9	#22F1D
3.10 CONTINUE	#1058A	#105C7	#22EF0
3.10 Program to make 'R/S' name	7C620	76C20	76C20
	A0F72	CEF72	0D9E0

		43F72	61082	CF9E0
		21D20	21D20	21D20
		30	30	30
		25F235	25F235	25F235
		E4F72	03082	71AE0
		F1F72	10082	6E9E0
		09F20	09F20	09F20
3.11	NEXT (Warning: the program expects at least one object on the stack, but it does not use the object.)	#E514	#E52A	#20256
3.11	MENU command	#E38E	#E3A4	Built-in command
3.11	Generating an integer	#6D56	#6D56	#71A9
3.12	NAME	#30064	#17564	not found
3.13	EDIT The HP-28S requires 4 SYSEVALs to be executed one after another for EDIT to be used in a program.	#C407	#C3FF	#1BFEB #189E7 #204A #1C009

4.1   The code and addresses are given only as an example and do not necessarily represent real addresses in any particular version.

4.2   The HP-28S manuals are even stricter in their demands that copyright not be infringed, so I have avoided giving any disassembled HP-28S code either.

4.3	Just change RAM top position (and use HOME on the HP-28S).	#4FFF2	#4FFF2	#CFFF2
4.4	Again change RAM top positions, e.g. as shown here for the PEEK program itself.	#4FF7B #4FFF0 #4FF76	#4FF7B #4FFF0 #4FF76	#CFF7B #CFFF0 #CFF76

4.4   The version messages begin at   #3FE7A   #3FF9B   #3FF97

4.5   See above for version number message.

      "CONTINUE"   #FCCF   #FCE5   #2263D

      CONTINUE code   #FCDF   #FCF5   #2264D

4.6 As in point 4.4 replace 4FF with CFF throughout.

      32 bit part of clock   #407F8   #407F8   #FFFF8
      (top of display RAM)

      48 bit part of clock   #4F003   #4F003   #C0003
      (at bottom of user RAM)

4.7   JMPM, JMPR   #4FFF9   #4FFF9   #CFFF9
      Again use top of RAM   #4FFF4   #4FFF4   #CFFF4
      (and HOME on HP-28S).   etc.   etc.   etc.

      NEXT study   #E530   #E532   #20252
      The HP-28S behaves differently! etc.   etc.   etc.

4.8   Key buffer begins at: #4F038   #4F038   #C0038
      (unless you have added memory).

INDEX

+CMD, 67
/O
  lack of, 118
1LG8, 124
ABORT, 31
Adding RAM, 134
ADDL, 23, 146
Address 0, 74
Addresses, 54
ALGEBRA, 45
Algebra with binary numbers, 42
Algebraic entry, 11
Algebraic entry like algebraic calculators, 13
Algebraic entry mode, 6
Algebraic expressions, 28
Alpha entry, 12
Alpha entry like BASIC, 13
Alpha entry mode, 6
Answering, 78
AREUH, 88
Argument, 8
ASCII, 14, 57, 63, 70
Asking questions, 33
Assembler, 87
Assemblers, 88
Assembly language programs, 88
ATTN, 3, 6

Bailey B., 40, 59, 168
Baker J., 180
Ball J. A., 157
Barcodes, 37
BASIC, 102

Batteries, 161
BCD, 63
BEEP, 61
Bender, 128
BIN, 47
Binary Coded Decimal, 63
Binary integers, 47
Binary masking, 42
Binary numbers, 42
BIP, 61
Breaking in, 127
Bugs, 74, 162, 163, 164, 166
Byte, 14, 57

Capacitors, 132
Casio, 42
CATALOG, 3, 5
Cawsey
  Graeme, 45,179
CDE, 116
Central Processor Unit, 81
Character, 14
Charcter 0, 14
CHHU Chronicle, 137
Choice of answers, 78
CHR, 36
CHR(0), 14
CHS bug in EDIT and VISIT, 164
Circuit board, 129
CLEAR, 45
CLMF, 49
CLOCK, 52
Clock corrections, 106
CLUSR, 45
CLX, 11

Cmof, 61
Cmon, 61
CMT, 126
COD, 70, 91
Code, 81, 116
Collinson A., 163, 204
Colon, 36
Comm, 60
Comma, 7
COMMAND, 5, 7, 10, 19, 47, 59
Command line, 10, 13, 14
Command names, 63
COMMAND
  as an alternative to
  programs, 10
Commands, 171
Commencement of a program, 110
Compilers, 88
Compiling, 39, 72
Complex arrays, 41
Complex numbers, 41
Conclusion of a program, 110
Configuration, 126
Confusing actions, 161
CONST, 56
Constants, 17
CONT, 31
CONTINUE, 100
CONTL, 148
Controller, 124
Copyright, 87
Copyright notice, 99
Correcting errors, 7
Courbis P., 174, 177, 179
CPU, 54, 81, 83, 84, 130, 180
CPU registers, 182
Cracknell M., 205

Crowther C., 137
Currencies, 7
Current directory, 140
Current menu, 3
Current path, 140
Cursor, 3, 13
Custom error messages, 61
Customized names, 58

D0, 84
D1, 84
Daisy chain input, 131
Daisy chain output, 131
Data objects, 14, 171
DATAFILE, 157
David P., 88
Debugging, 31
DECOD, 101
Decompilers, 88
Decompiling, 39
Decompiling system objects, 89
DEG, 6
DELL, 151
DEPTH, 8
Diagnostic module, 48
Direct commands, 8
Direct I/O connection, 131
Display, 74
Display layout and control,
  130
Dodin
  Jean-Daniel, 40,59
Dot, 7
Drilling in, 128
DROP, 10
Drop tests, 125
DROPN, 8

Dummy, 94
Dummy variables, 144
DUP, 8
Duplicate names, 144
Duplicate variables, 142

E, 17, 41
EDIT, 13, 77
EduCALC, 126, 137, 157
EEX bug in EDIT and VISIT, 164
Electronic notebook, 144
ELSE, 25
END, 25
ENG, 6
ENTER, 3, 5, 8, 13, 14
ENTER and the command line, 14
Entry modes, 6, 11, 13
Error messages, 61, 62
Error recovery, 7
Errors, 13
EVAL, 5, 10
EVEN, 68, 91
Examining RAM, 100
Example books, 155
Examples, 1
Execute, 88
Extend Your HP-41, 157
Extra RAM, 157
Ezra R., 137

FACT, 25, 32
Faults, 161
FBYTE, 69, 91
FETCH, 3
Field, 183
Filler, 98
Filler bytes, 98

FINDL, 147
FIX, 6
Flag 31, 9
Flag 60, 26
Flags, 15
Flags 57 58 and 59, 60
FOR...STEP, 34
FORM, 45
FORTH, 77, 90, 155
FORTH/Assembler module, 88, 90

G, 17
Garbage collection, 50, 114,
    133
Generalized ->STR, 57
Generalized STO, 56
GET, 24
GETI, 24
Getting Started manual, 1
Global and local names, 41
Global names, 175
Global variables, 38, 142
GOLONG, 92
GOVLNG, 92
Grapevine Publications, 156

HALT, 31
Hang-up, 54, 118
Hard addressing, 126
Hardware, 54
Harvey R., 157
HEX, 47
Hexadecimal integers, 47
High-level languages, 88
Holm K., 137
Holm
    Kim, 119

Home directory, 139
Hook-uP, 132, 157
HP calculators, 1
HP Journal, 130, 137
HP-15C, 156
HP-15C Advanced
  Functions Handbook, 156
HP-16C, 42
HP-18, 54, 86
HP-18C, 125
HP-19, 86
HP-28 assembler, 89
HP-28 disassembler, 89
HP-28 INSIGHTS (book), 156
HP-28 mini-assembler, 89
HP-28C, 47
HP-28C subdirectories, 143
HP-28S, 17, 29, 30, 47
HP-28S RAM and ROM
  positions, 179
HP-28S subdirectories, 17
HP-41, 6, 34, 37, 43, 48,
  68, 203
HP-71, 6, 48
HP-71B, 54, 74, 84,
  124, 126, 156
HP-71B assembler, 88
HP-71B FORTH/Assembler
  module, 89
HP-71B IDS, 87
HP-71B internal design
specification, 54
HP-71B memory modules, 126
HP-82240A printer, 1
HPCC, 124, 157
HPX, 157, 163
Hybrid, 124

I, 17, 41
Ian Maw, 56
Ianization, 59, 85
IBM PCs, 88
IDS, 54, 87, 130, 155
IF, 25
IFTE, 27, 28
Immediate entry, 11
Immediate entry like RPN
  calculators, 13
Immediate entry mode, 6
In-line code, 118
In-line machine code, 112
Indirect addressing, 84
Indirect commands, 8
Inductor, 132
Infra-red transmitter bulb,
  131
Insert mode, 6
Instruction, 83
Instruction pointer, 90
Integers, 74
Interfacing, 132
Interpreters, 88
INTOFF, 91
INTOFF program, 91
INTON program, 92
IP, 23
IP and Ip, 46

J, 41
Janick Taillandier, 88
Jean-Daniel Dodin, 59
JMPM, 111
JMPR, 112, 116
Jumping into a machine
  language program, 110

Jumping into an RPL program, 112

Jumping into programs, 110

Key buffer, 119

Keyboards, 3

Keycodes, 119

Keys, 91

KILL, 31

Kim Holm, 119

Labels, 123

Lambda variables, 86

LAST, 7, 59

LC, 23

Leather case, 123

Leather cases, 157

Lennaerts M., 5

LISP, 86

Local and ordinary (global) names, 41

Local names, 175

Local variables, 24, 26, 27, 38, 142

Loop, 34

Looping and the stack, 34

Low-level languages, 88

Lower case, 23, 119

Lower case letters, 41

Machine code, 81

Machine language, 81

Machine language programs, 88

Machine instructions, 81

Madsen F., 5

Manuals, 1, 155, 203, 205

MASK, 42

Masking, 42

Matrices, 19

Maw I., 137

MAXR, 17

MEM, 45

Memory, 13, 65, 124

Memory layout, 65

Memory Lost, 52, 118

Memory reset, 52, 54

MENU, 45, 76

Menu layout example, 138

Menu numbers, 75

Menus, 45, 74

Microcomputer interface, 132

Mini-disassembler, 89

MINR, 17

Mnemonic, 83

Mnemonics, 87, 183

Modes, 5, 35

Modifier, 183

Modifiers, 91, 93

Modules, 37

MS-DOS, 88

NAME, 77

Negative exponents, 63

Nelson R., 155

New versions, 203

NEWLINE, 145, 168

NEXT, 45, 74

Niemeijer M., 174

NIP, 21, 22, 81

NNC, 70, 91

NNN, 66, 67

NNNs, 64

NNO, 67, 70

Non-keyable characters, 36

Non-Normalized name, 72
Non-Normalized numbers, 63
Non-Normalized objects, 67
Notebook, 1, 152
NRCL, 42
NSTO, 42
NSWP, 44
Null, 14
NUM, 85
Numbered registers, 42
NXT, 74
Nybble, 57

Object storage, 172
Objects -their structure, 171
ON, 3
One-command programs, 45
Operating System, 55
Operation, 19
Ordinary and local names, 41
Ordinary or global names, 40
Ordinary variables, 142
Out of Memory, 30, 44
OVER, 8, 44

P, 141
P command for moving between
  directories, 141
Paris club, 88
PC interface, 157
PC=(A), 84, 85
PCB, 135
PEEK, 96, 116
Petersen S., 5, 77
Phantom } bug, 166
Pi, 11, 17
PICK, 8, 11, 43

Pierre David, 88
Pin connections, 131
PLACE, 43
Plotting, 161
Point, 7
Pointer registers, 90
Pointers, 90
POKE, 102, 104, 116, 119
Position independent code, 113
PREV, 45, 119
Printer, 1, 3
Printer control flags, 16
PRMD, 6
PRMT, 33
Problems, 161
Program control of COMMAND, 61
Program control of LAST, 61
Programmable EDIT, 77
Programs, 20
Programs - their structure,
  171
Prolog, 171
PROMPT, 34
Prompting, 33
PRVAR, 9
Pseudo-operations, 87
Pseudo-ops, 87
PURGE, 32, 45
PURGE
  a warning, 98

Quadratic, 18

R/S, 68, 71
RAD, 6
Radix, 7
Radix mode, 7

RAM, 55, 124
RCL, 39
RCLF, 35
RDZ, 49
Reference manual, 1
Register 0, 42
Replace mode, 6
Residual array, 32
Result string, 69, 101
Return stack, 84
Reverse Polish Notation, 86
Ripple, 87
RND bug, 164
ROLL, 8
ROLLD, 8
ROM, 55, 124
ROM-based Procedural
    Language, 87
ROMAN 8, 14
Roots, 18
ROT, 8
Routines, 33
RPL, 86, 90, 155
RPN, 86, 90
RSD, 32
Rules
    for local and ordinary
    (global) names, 41
Run, 88
RUSH systems, 132, 157

Saturn, 54, 83, 124
Saturn assemblers, 88
Saturn CPU, 180
Saving space, 32
Schwartz J., 204
SCI, 6

Self-reference, 168
Separator, 7
SETM, 35
Sharing local variables, 40
SHIFT, 3
Short programs, 30
Signals, 131
SINC, 33
Smith J., 137
Soft addressing, 126
Solution Books, 1
SOLVR, 45
Source string, 69, 101
Space saving, 32
Special characters, 37
Speeding-up, 133
SRCHL, 148
SST, 31, 71
Stack, 8, 38
Stack analysis form, 26
Stack operations, 114
Stack pointer, 90
START...NEXT, 34
STD, 6
Steen Petersen, 77
Stefano Tendon, 88
Step, 83
STO, 18, 56, 58
STOF, 35
STRING, 14, 82
String comparison bug, 164
Subdirectories, 30, 139
Submenus, 139
Subprogram, 82
Subprograms, 30, 33
Suspended program, 31
SWAP, 8

Synthetic Programming, 37, 48
Synthetic registers, 43
SYNTHETIX, 157
SYSEVAL, 5, 46, 47, 54, 108
SYSEVAL evaluation, 74
System clock, 49, 105
System Halt, 54, 74
System Object, 59, 89, 118
System Objects, 74

Taillandier J., 88
Technical Notes, 157
Temporary variables, 142
Tendon S., 88
THEN, 25
Thread, 82, 84
Thread pointer, 112
Threaded interpreter, 86
Threaded language, 86
TI, 42
TIME, 51
Time-out, 105
Time-out
  disabling, 105
Timer circuit, 132
Timer circuits, 133
Timings, 49
Top of memory, 65, 70
TUCK, 21
Turbo-71, 88

UDF, 28
UNDO, 7, 9, 59, 60, 161
Unof, 61
Unon, 61
UP program, 141
USER, 6, 44

User club addresses, 158
User clubs, 48, 152, 157
User groups, 56
USER menu, 20
User mode, 6
User-defined function, 28
User-written commands, 21
Using SYSEVAL, 108

Variables, 18
VER$, 48
Version 1BB, 48, 203
Version 1CC, 48, 203
Version 2BB, 48, 203
Version numbers, 47
VIEW, 5
VISIT, 11, 39, 43

Wales F., 162
Walsh B., 163, 204
White D., 137
Wickes
  Dr.Bill, 40,55,156

XTOA, 37

YES key bug, 165
YES/NO, 33

Zengrange, 126, 137

THE PHOTOGRAPHS

The photographs should give you some idea of how to open an HP-28C and what is inside it. The circuits inside the HP-28S or other new models will not be exactly the same. Photo 1 shows an HP-28C with the stick-down overlays on the keyboard and above the display removed. You should be able to see a row of holes above the display, with the peg-tops in the middle of each hole. The keyboard is held down by more such pegs: you have drill out the top of every one to be able to open an HP-28.

Photo 2 shows the right-hand part of the HP-28C after it has been opened up. The circuit board is clearly seen, above the keyboard (the keys have been removed) and below the battery compartment. If the three 1.5V batteries were replaced by a single smaller battery then the space freed by the other two could be used to hold plug-in modules or I/O devices. The keys normally sit on a thin rubber mat which lies on top of the keyboard "sandwich" - this rubber mat has been removed so you can see the metal foil which detects keystrokes. The circle above the keyboard, stuck inside the back of the case, is the "bender" which makes the BEEP sounds.

Photo 3 is an enlargement of the circuit board seen in photo 2. In the top right corner is the infra red bulb used to send signals to the printer - the bulb is not clearly seen in the photograph as it is transparent. To the left of the bulb, and lower down, is the capacitor used to support the constant memory while the batteries are being changed. Below this capacitor is the inductor used in the CPU timer, and the two capacitors used for this timer are to the left of the inductor. Other surface mounted components can be seen on the board, the most interesting are the two hybrids at the left and right - marked 1LP3-0016 and 1LP3-0015. The numbers and letters below these identifiers are the date and place of manufacture (Singapore). These hybrids carry the HP-28C ROM. Along the bottom are the keyboard contacts. To the left of the middle are two springs which connect to the bender.

Photo 4 shows the inside of an HP-71B 4K ROM plug-in module, enlarged to roughly the same scale as photo 3. The inside of a RAM module looks very similar.

PHOTO 1

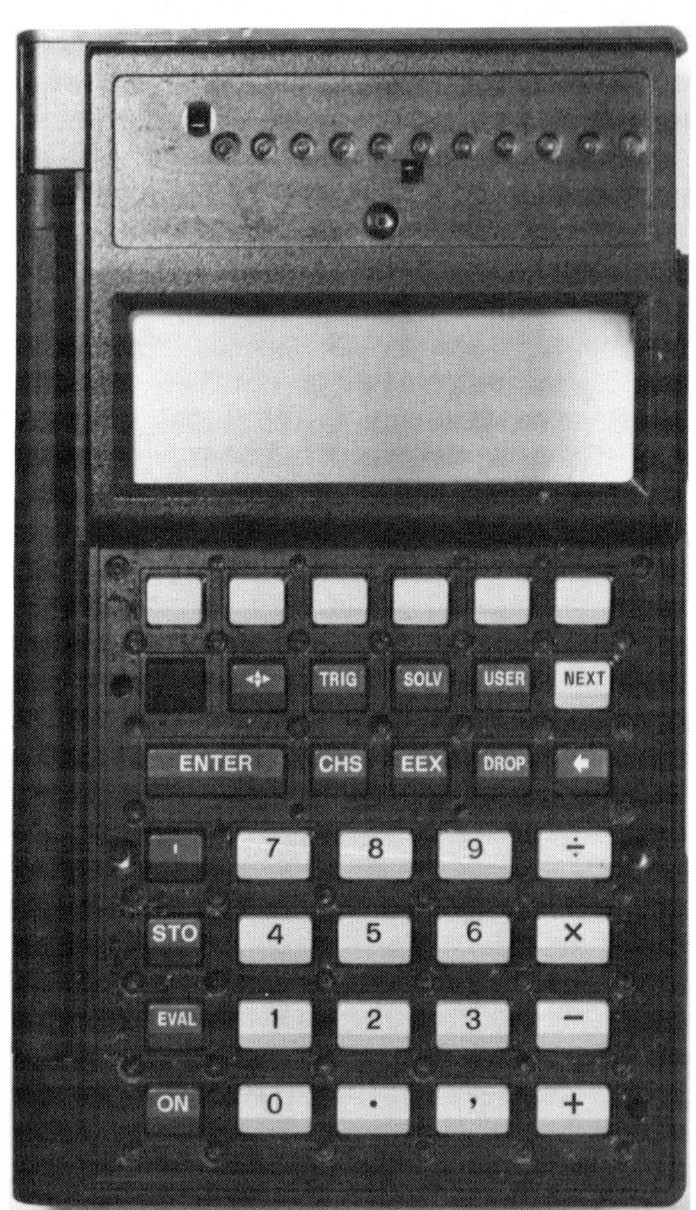

PHOTO 2

PHOTO 4

PHOTO 3

Rotated 90 degrees clockwise with reference to Photo 2

ORDER BLANK

	Price per copy	Qty	Amount

<u>For HP-28C's</u> & <u>HP-28S's</u>
Customize Your HP-28, by W.A.C. Mier-Jedrzejowicz — $16.95

<u>For HP-71'S</u>
HP-71 Basic Made Easy, by Joseph Horn — $18.95

<u>For HP-71'S</u> & <u>HP-41'S</u>
Control the World with HP-IL, by Gary Friedman — $24.95

<u>For HP-41'S</u>
HP-41 Advanced Programming Tips, by A. McCornack & K. Jarett — $20.95

HP-41 M-Code for Beginners, by Ken Emery — $24.95

Inside the HP-41, by Jean-Daniel Dodin — $12.95

Extend Your HP-41, by W.A.C. Mier-Jędrzejowicz — $29.95

HP-41 Extended Functions Made Easy, by Keith Jarett — $16.95

HP-41 Synthetic Programming Made Easy, by Keith Jarett — $16.95
(Includes one Quick Reference Card)

Quick Reference Card for Synthetic Programming — $2.00

Synthetic Quick Reference Guide (SQRG) — $5.95

<u>Humor</u>
**It's Amazing How These Things Can Simplify Your Life:
The Harold Guide to Computer Literacy** — $4.95

<u>ROM's</u>
SKWIDBC -- Barcode Generation Module by Ken Emery — $199.95

SKWIDBC Plus -- for LaserJet Plus or Series II — $199.95
(Upgrade from SKWIDBC for <u>$50</u> plus SKWIDBC tradein)

AECROM by Redshift Software — $ 99.00

Sales tax (California orders only, 6 or 7%)

Shipping	1st book	Add'l books
within USA, book rate (4th class)	$1.50	$0.50
USA 48 states, United Parcel Service	$2.50	$1.00
USA, Canada, air mail	$3.00	$1.50
elsewhere, book rate (6 to 8 week wait)	$2.00	$1.00
elsewhere, air mail	$12.05 for **Extend Your HP-41**, $6.05 for others	

<u>Free</u> shipping for **It's Amazing...** with purchase of any other book
<u>Free</u> shipping for **ROM's, QRC** plastic cards or **SQRG** (any number)

Enter shipping total here — $________

Total due — $________

Checks must be in U.S. funds, and payable through a U.S. bank.

Name________________________________
Address_____________________________

City____________________State________Zipcode____________
Country_____________________________

Mail to:
SYNTHETIX, P.O.Box 1080, Berkeley, CA 94701-1080, USA   Phone (415) 339-0601